International Rules of Law Relating to Bills of Lading

Comprising: — The Harter Act, 1893 — The Hague Rules, 1924 — The Visby Rules, 1963 — The Brussels Protocol, 1968 — The Hague Rules 1924 as amended by the Brussels Protocol 1968 — The Carriage of Goods by Sea Act 1971 — The Hamburg Rules, 1978 — together with a brief introduction and historical background to each.

D1205185

Fairplay Publications

Published and distributed by
FAIRPLAY PUBLICATIONS LTD.
20 Ullswater Crescent, Coulsdon Business Estate
Coulsdon, Surrey CR3 2HR, United Kingdom
Telephone: 01-660 2811
Fax: 01-660 2824
Telex: 884595 FRPLAY G

ISBN 0 905045 34 3

Copyright © 1982 by Fairplay Publications Ltd.

Front cover: Photo by Ambrose Greenway.

First Published July 1982
Reprinted December 1988

Typeset by JJ Typographics, Rochford, Essex.

Printed by Mayhew McCrimmon Printers Ltd., Gt. Wakering, Essex.

Author's Preface

WHEN the International Convention for the unification of certain rules of law relating to bills of lading was signed at Brussels on the 25th August 1924, adopting the Hague Rules, the intention was that the Rules should become mandatory and apply to bills of lading worldwide. Although this was not achieved, and although to this day there are a number of maritime nations who have not adopted the Rules nor given effect to them in their internal legislation, nevertheless the great majority of nations have done so. And, with many nations making the Rules applicable to bills of lading covering cargo shipped to or from their ports, the Rules have in fact achieved almost universal application to bills of lading issued throughout the world.

However, over the past few decades events have taken place leading to amendments to the Rules, namely the Visby Rules, 1963, the Brussels Protocol 1968 (Hague-Visby Rules), and the Hamburg Rules, 1978, the intention of the latter being to replace the Hague Rules, the Visby Rules and the Hague-Visby Rules. But present indications are that because these Rules only become effective between contracting States as and when they ratify the Conventions and introduce internal legislation to give the Rules statutory effect (such as the introduction of the Carriage of Goods by Sea Act, 1971, in the United Kingdom giving effect to the Hague-Visby Rules) no one set of Rules will have universal application.

So it is that commercial people concerned with the business of the carriage of goods by sea, i.e. shipowners, cargo owners and their respective insurers, will, in the day-to-day business of the adjustment of claims arising out of cargo loss or damage, and the determination of the question of the liability of the carrier under the contract of carriage evidenced by the bill of lading, have need to determine in the first place which particular set of international rules of law govern the terms and conditions of the bill of lading. Having determined that issue, then the parties must of necessity refer to those Rules.

The author has here provided in one compact volume an immediate reference to all the international rules relating to matters of liability for cargo loss or damage during the course of ocean transport under contracts evidenced by bills of lading, so avoiding the need to seek out the individual laws in order to ascertain their relevance to the issues of liability in respect of cargo loss or damage arising under the bill of lading. Additionally there is provided a succinctly stated resume of the events leading to each of the individual international rules of law relating to contracts evidenced by bills of lading.

For these reasons it is hoped that this present work will be welcomed not only by commercial interests but also by the legal profession, who will now have in one volume all the international laws relative to bills of lading. Last, but not least, the book should be of value to students taking examinations and those entering into this field of maritime law.

An in-depth study of the effect and interpretation of these maritime rules will be found in the following books by the same author:-

Shipping and the Law

An explanatory work covering the interpretation and effect of the Hague Rules and the Hague Rules as amended by the Visby Rules in the day-to-day business of the settlement of claims arising under contracts for the carriage of goods by sea evidenced by bills of lading.

Hague Rules Law Digest

A companion volume to **Shipping and the Law**, providing a ready reference to the leading British law cases involving decisions on the effect and interpretation of the Rules on numerous problems of law arising thereunder.

The Hamburg Rules

An explanation of the cause and effect of the Rules together with an immediate rule-by-rule comparison with the relative Hague Rule and a detailed explanation of the nature and manner of the amendments to the Hague Rules and the Hague-Visby Rules.

INTRODUCTION

IN the day-to-day business of the handling of problems of liability for cargo loss or damage occurring during the course of sea carriage, shipowners, charterers and other carriers on the one hand, and cargo interests and their respective insurers on the other, will need to have available, for constant reference, the international rules of law relative to bills of lading and similar contracts of carriage. Although such rules are only statutorily applicable to contracts evidenced by bills of lading or other similar documents of title, they are commonly made applicable to charter parties, and other contracts for the carriage of goods by sea, by way of voluntary incorporation into the terms of such contracts.

It follows therefore that when cargo suffers loss or damage during the course of transport by sea, the question of the liability of the carrier will almost certainly need to be determined in accordance with such international rules. Presently operative in this particular field of seaborne commerce are the Hague Rules as agreed at the International Convention for the unification of certain rules of law relating to bills of lading signed at Brussels on the 25th August, 1924; The Hague-Visby Rules, as amended by the Brussels Protocol, 1968, signed at Brussels in February, 1968, following upon the 1967-68 session of the Diplomatic Conference on Maritime Law; and certain provisions of the Harter Act of the United States which dates back to 1893. More recently we have the Hamburg Rules agreed at the United Nations Conference of the Carriage of Goods by Sea, March, 1978, which Rules have yet to come into effect, but will come into force from the date of the 20th instrument of ratification, acceptance, approval or accession.

In the years following upon the Brussels International Convention of 1924, maritime nations proceeded to give effect to the Hague Rules by the introduction of the necessary legislation in their codes of commerce or statute books. Those Rules of Law have now been universally accepted to the extent of voluntary incorporation in contracts to which the Rules do not statutorily apply, seemingly being recognised as a fair and equitable disposition of the risks of cargo loss or damage to be borne by cargo interests on the one hand and shipowning interests on the other.

This was indeed a happy state of affairs for commercial people because throughout the world of seaborne commerce, cargo and shipowning interests knew exactly where they stood as regards liability for cargo loss or damage arising under contracts of carriage evidenced by bills of lading worldwide or under other contracts in which the rules had been incorporated. However, in June, 1963, at the Stockholm Conference of the

Comite Maritime International it was proposed that the Hague Rules should be amended in certain respects but complete agreement was not reached. This led to a Diplomatic Conference on Maritime Law 1967-1968 following upon which there was signed at Brussels in 1968 a Protocol amending the Hague Rules in certain respects. Although this Protocol was given effect in the United Kingdom by the passing of the Carriage of Goods by Sea Act, 1971, it will be a long time (if ever) before all the maritime nations of the world take similar action. But in the meantime, the Hamburg Rules were agreed at the United Nations Conference on the Carriage of Goods by Sea, March, 1978, and again it is far from certain that all maritime nations will ratify the rules and give them legal effect.

So it seems that for a very long time to come cargo interests and shipowning interests and their respective insurers, in resolving questions of liability for cargo loss or damage, will need to have before them, for immediate reference, the Hague Rules as agreed at the Brussels International Convention in 1924; the Hague Rules as amended by the Brussels Protocol 1968 (the Hague-Visby Rules); the Hamburg Rules, March 1978; the Harter Act of 1893, and, the Visby Rules June, 1963.

CONTENTS

The Rules of Law relating to bills of lading traced through the years from the introduction of the Harter Act of the United States, 1893 to the Final Act of the United Nations introducing the Hamburg Rules, March, 1978.

	Page No.
Events leading to the Harter Act of the United States, 1893	9
The Harter Act, 1893	11
Events leading to the Hague Rules, 1924	13
The Hague Rules, 1924	17
Events leading to the Visby Rules, 1963	25
The Visby Rules, 1963	28
Events leading to the Brussels Protocol, 1968 (Hague/Visby Rules)	30
Brussels Protocol, 1968	31
The Hague — Visby Rules (The Hague Rules, 1924, as amended by the Brussels Protocol, 1968)	37
Events leading to the Carriage of Goods by Sea Act, 1971, giving effect to the Hague Rules as amended by the Brussels Protocol, 1968	44
Carriage of Goods by Sea Act, 1971	46
Events leading to the Hamburg Rules, 1978	49
The Hamburg Rules, 1978	52

Events leading to the Harter Act of the United States, 1893 — Approved February 13, 1893 — Effective after the first day of July, 1893

THE precursor of international law relating to the carriage of goods by sea, under contracts evidenced by bills of lading, is generally recognised as the Harter Act of 1893. The passing of this Act by U.S. Congress in 1893 led to similar enactments being introduced, at the turn of the century, by a number of the British Commonwealth nations, including Australia, Canada and New Zealand, followed by the Dominions Royal Commission instituting an enquiry into the position. And in 1920 the Imperial Government appointed an Imperial Shipping Committee to review the position relative to the liability of the carrier for cargo loss or damage suffered during the carriage of goods by sea. In the report of that Committee, issued in 1921, the recommendation was made that there should be uniform legislation throughout the Commonwealth, based upon the American Harter Act of 1893. Shortly after this, the Maritime Law Committee of the International Law Association was requested to submit a draft code of rules to the full conference to be held at the Hague in September, 1921, which led eventually to the introduction of the Hague Rules.

When considering the events leading to the introduction of the Harter Act, it is necessary to have in mind the tremendous growth in seaborne commerce which took place during the nineteenth century, during which time (prior to the Harter Act) shipowners generally had great freedom of contract as to the terms and conditions under which goods might be carried.

In the early days of the 19th century shipowners generally were not inclined to take undue advantage of this freedom but, as the century progressed and commerce was developing rapidly, shipowners began to limit their stringent liabilities for loss or damage to cargo by inserting exculpatory clauses in their bills of lading. Some shipowners began to include clauses in their bills of lading exonerating themselves from liability for cargo loss or damage in certain specified circumstances, but other clauses came to be introduced having the effect of relieving the owners from liability for cargo loss or damage arising or resulting from the shipowners' own negligence or the negligence of his agents or servants.

Clauses exempting the shipowner from liability for cargo loss or damage arising or resulting from the unseaworthiness of the vessel began to be introduced, eventually leading to a situation in which the shipowner was achieving almost complete immunity from cargo loss or damage however caused. Shipowners held great bargaining powers which they began to wield to their benefit in their trading conditions, to the detriment of the cargo interests, who were virtually powerless to fight against the inclusion of these wide exculpatory clauses in their bills of lading. Bills of lading consequently became contracts of adhesion forced upon shippers by shipowners and carriers of goods by sea.

The United States Congress felt compelled to act to prevent this abuse of the freedom of contract enjoyed by shipowners and other carriers of goods by sea and, in the result, there emerged the Harter Act of 1893. Under Section I of the Act it was unlawful for the owner of any vessel, or her manager, agent or master, transporting merchandise or property from or between ports of the United States and foreign ports, to insert in any bill of lading any clause whereby it, he or they would be relieved from liability for loss or damage arising from negligence, fault, or failure in proper loading, stowage, custody, care, or proper delivery of property committed to its charge.

Section 2 of the Act provided, amongst other things that it was unlawful for any such vessel, her owner, master or agent, or manager to insert in any bill of lading any covenant or agreement whereby the obligations of the owner or owners of the vessel to exercise due diligence, properly equip, man, provision, and outfit the vessel, and to make the vessel seaworthy and capable of performing her intended voyage, or whereby the obligations of the master, officers, agents, or servants to carefully handle and stow her cargo and to care for and properly deliver same, should in any wise be lessened, weakened, or avoided.

The Act was effective whether the ship was under United States ownership or under foreign ownership, and, most importantly, it was applicable to vessels carrying goods to or from ports of the United States. It should be further noted that whilst this Act was largely superseded when the United States gave effect to the Hague Rules by the passing of the U.S. Carriage of Goods by Sea Act in 1936, it is still applicable to the period following upon the discharge of the goods from the ship until proper delivery has been effected. The Harter Act applies as soon as the cargo has left the ship's tackle and, from that time until proper delivery has been completed, no exculpatory clause in the bill of lading can save the shipowner from any liability arising out of failure to care properly for the cargo or to make proper delivery. Unfortunately "proper delivery" is not defined in the Act, and must therefore be determined by the circumstances of the individual case concerned. But certainly discharge of the goods from the vessel cannot in all circumstances be equated with proper delivery.

Section 3 of the Act has the effect of making exemptions from liability for cargo loss or damage, subject to the shipowner having exercised due diligence to make the ship seaworthy. One further point that should be mentioned is that the Harter Act does not require a causal connection between unseaworthiness and damage to cargo, whereas the United States Carriage of Goods by Sea Act, which gives effect to the Hague Rules, does.

Not only was the Harter Act the forerunner of international law relative to the carriage of goods by sea under contracts evidenced by bills of lading, but it was also the basis upon which later laws of maritime nations were drafted, and in fact laid down the basis for the Hague Rules.

THE HARTER ACT OF THE UNITED STATES, 1893

An Act relating to navigation of vessels, bills of lading, and to certain obligations, duties and rights in connection with the carriage of property.

Be it enacted by the Senate and House of Representatives of the United States of America in Congress assembled, That

Sect. 1. It shall not be lawful for the manager, agent, master, or owner of any vessel transporting merchandise or property from or between ports of the United States and foreign ports to insert in any bill of lading or shipping document any clause, covenant, or agreement whereby it, he, or they shall be relieved from liability for loss or damage arising from negligence, fault, or failure in proper loading, stowage, custody, care, or proper delivery of any and all lawful merchandise or property committed to its or their charge. Any and all words or clauses of such import inserted in bills of lading or shipping receipts shall be null and void and of no effect.

Sect. 2. It shall not be lawful for any vessel transporting merchandise or property from or between ports of the United States of America and foreign ports, her owner, master, agent, or manager, to insert in any bill of lading or shipping document any covenant or agreement whereby the obligations of the owner or owners of said vessel, to exercise due diligence, properly equip, man, provision, and outfit said vessel, and to make said vessel seaworthy and capable of performing her intended voyage, or whereby the obligations of the master, officers, agents, or servants to carefully handle and stow her cargo and to care for and properly deliver same, shall in any wise be lessened, weakened, or avoided.

Sect. 3. If the owner of any vessel transporting merchandise or property to or from any port in the United States of America shall exercise due diligence to make the said vessel in all respects seaworthy and properly manned, equipped, and supplied, neither the vessel, her owner or owners, agent, or charterers shall become or be held responsible for damage or loss resulting from faults or errors in navigation or in the management of said vessel nor shall the vessel, her owner or owners, charterers, agent or master be held liable for losses arising from dangers of the sea or other navigable waters, acts of God, or public enemies, or the inherent defect, quality, or vice of the thing carried, or from insufficiency of package or seizure under legal process, or for loss resulting from any act or omission of the shipper or owner of the goods, his agent or representative, or from saving or attempting to save life or property at sea, or from any deviation in rendering such service.

Sect. 4. It shall be the duty of the owner or owners, master or agent of any vessel transporting merchandise or property from or between ports of the United States or foreign ports to issue to shippers of any lawful merchandise a bill of lading, or shipping document, stating, among other things, the marks necessary for identification, number of packages, or quantity, stating whether it be carrier's or shipper's weight, and apparent order or condition of such merchandise or property delivered to and received by the owner, master, or agent of the vessel for transportation, and such document shall be *prima facie* evidence of the receipt of merchandise therein described.

Sect. 5. For a violation of any of the provisions of this act the agent, owner, or master of the vessel guilty of such violation and who refuses to issue on demand the bill of lading herein provided for, shall be liable to a fine not exceeding two thousand dollars. The amount of the fine and costs for such violation shall be a lien upon the vessel, whose agent, owner, or master is guilty of such violation, and such vessel may be libelled therefore in any district court in the United States, within whose jurisdiction the vessel may be found. One-half of such penalty shall go to the party injured by such violation and the remainder to the Government of the United States.

Sect. 6. This Act shall not be held to modify or repeal sections forty-two hundred and eighty-one, forty-two hundred and eighty-two, and forty-two hundred and eighty-three of the Revised Statutes of the United States, or any other statute defining the liability of the vessels, their owners, or representatives.

Sect. 7. Sections one and four of this Act shall not apply to the transportation of live animals.

Sect. 8. This Act shall take effect from and after the first day of July, eighteen hundred and ninety-three.

Approved, February 13, 1893.

Events leading to the Hague Rules as agreed at the International Convention for the unification of certain rules of law signed at Brussels on the 25th August, 1924.

HISTORICALLY, maritime law was such that the carrier of goods by sea was held liable for any loss or damage suffered by the cargo during the voyage regardless of the cause of such loss or damage and whether or not it resulted from the negligence of the carrier. The only exceptions to this rule were losses caused by act of God, public enemies, inherent vice of the goods themselves, fault of the shipper, or losses suffered by a general average sacrifice. But even then the carrier would become liable if he had been negligent or otherwise at fault. In order to recover the value of any cargo loss or damage suffered by the goods during the voyage, the cargo owner would need only to prove that the carrier received the goods on board the vessel in good order and condition and prove either the bad order of the goods or non-delivery at the place of discharge. There was also implied in all contracts for the carriage of goods by sea an obligation that the vessel was seaworthy.

The shipowner's liability under common law and civil law codes was in theory very strict, and shipowners and cargo interests generally seem to have been in agreement that it was the responsibility of the shipowner to carry and deliver the goods to the port of discharge in the same apparent order in which they were shipped or otherwise make good any loss suffered by the cargo owner by reason of any loss or damage that the goods had sustained. So, with the benefit of hindsight, it can be seen that (maybe unwittingly at the time) a maritime code of rules governing the carriage of goods by sea was being formed.

It is necessary to digress for a moment to look at the events leading to the bill of lading. In the old days merchants would travel with their goods, the particulars of which would be entered in a book or register which was part of the ship's papers. But as trade developed, the merchant ceased to accompany his goods, and the necessity then arose for a separate document which was at first in the nature of a receipt for the goods but later became a document which embodied the terms on which the carrier would carry and deliver the goods at the port of destination. So was born the bill of lading which, in future years, was to develop into the negotiable document of present times.

In course of time the bill of lading became the basic shipping document, embodying or evidencing the contractual relationship between the carrier and the shipper, and taking the form of a non-negotiable bill of lading. But with the growth of seaborne commerce there came also an increasing need for the means of transferring the title in the goods before they arrived at destination. From this in turn arose the practice of transferring the ownership of the goods by endorsing the bill of lading to the buyer, and so the bill of lading as a negotiable document came into being.

These early bills of lading did not normally contain any clauses exempting the shipowner or carrier from liability for cargo loss or damage. But when cargo interests began in the latter part of the nineteenth century to take action against shipowners for the recovery of loss or damage to cargo occurring during the voyage, and to obtain legal rulings establishing the shipowners' liability for such loss or damage to their goods, shipowners generally sought to counter this by including in their bills of lading clauses exonerating them from liability for cargo loss or damage and so limiting contractually the strict liability imposed upon them by law.

Shipowners were entitled to do this by reason of the freedom of contract principles expressed in both the Common Law and Civil Law, shipowners and other carriers of goods by sea being so permitted by the laws of the land to extend those principles of freedom of contract to contracts evidenced by bills of lading issued in connection with the carriage of goods by sea.

These rights were generally exercised quite ruthlessly, and successfully, so that from a position where the shipowner or other carrier of goods by sea under contracts of carriage evidenced by bills of lading was virtually the insurer of the goods and responsible for any loss or damage sustained by the cargo, the situation was reversed. Hence the shipowner or carrier was exonerated from almost every liability for cargo loss or damage. If a Court decision went against the shipowners then that door would be immediately closed by including in the bill of lading a new clause giving the shipowner or carrier immunity from liability in the future.

The manner in which this right of freedom of contract was being exercised caused serious concern among the trading nations because overseas commerce was developing upon credit and bills of lading were the medium through which credits financing overseas commerce were arranged. And banking interests, quite apart from cargo interests, were being seriously affected by this right of the shipowner or other carrier to divest themselves of the responsibility of delivering the cargo at destination in sound condition or paying for any loss or damage that the cargo had suffered. The consignee would have bought the goods, and the bank would have advanced the money for purchase to the shipper upon the bill of lading issued acknowledging the shipment of the goods in apparent good order and condition. But the goods may have been delivered to the consignees in a worthless condition by reason, for example, of seawater entering the hold during the voyage due to the unseaworthiness of the vessel. The shipowner or carrier would deny any liability for the loss suffered by the consignee, pleading the exculpatory clauses contained in the bill of lading.

The negotiable bill of lading was in common use, and cargo and banking interests were complaining bitterly about the manner in which shipowners and carriers were (in their opinion) abusing the right of freedom of contract. The need for legislative action was recognised in the United States, when

Congress, in 1893, passed the Harter Act unifying the terms and conditions of contracts of carriage evidenced by bills of lading issued for the carriage of goods by sea to or from and between ports of the United States, so bringing to an end the right of shipowners and carriers to freedom of contract in respect of such voyages in connection with contracts evidenced by bills of lading.

The effect of that Act was, amongst other things, to render null and void any clauses in bills of lading relieving the shipowner or carrier from liability for loss or damage to cargo arising from negligence, fault, or failure in the proper loading, stowage, custody, care or proper delivery of the cargo. Also rendered null and void were any clauses contained in a bill of lading whereby the obligations of the shipowner to exercise due diligence, properly equip, man, provision, and make the ship seaworthy and capable of performing her intended voyage, or whereby the obligations of the master, officers, agents or servants to carefully handle and stow her cargo and to care for and deliver the same, should in any way be lessened, weakened or avoided. Further the Act required that the shipowner should exercise due diligence to make the vessel in all respects seaworthy and properly manned and equipped and supplied.

Subject to the owner of any vessel transporting merchandise or property to or from any port in the United States having exercised due diligence to make the vessel seaworthy, the Act gave the shipowner immunity from liability for, amongst other things, cargo loss or damage resulting from faults or errors in the navigation or management of the vessel, perils of the sea, acts of God, public enemies, inherent defect in the goods carried, insufficiency of packaging, deviation for the purpose of saving life or property at sea. These are but a few of the provisions of the Harter Act selected to illustrate the basic similarity between the provisions of that Act and the Hague Rules.

So, it might be said, were the foundations being laid for the Hague Rules, in that, largely built on this Act, there followed the Australian Sea Carriage of Goods Act, 1904, the Fiji Ordinance of 1906, the Canadian Water Carriage of Goods Act, 1910 and a series of Acts in New Zealand in 1908, 1911 and 1912 leading to the New Zealand Carriage of Goods by Sea Act 1922, which gave way eventually to the countries giving effect to legislation incorporating the Hague Rules.

In 1921 the Maritime Law Committee of the International Law Association held a meeting, when the views of both shipowning and cargo interests, in relation to proposals being put forward for the introduction of uniform legislation worldwide, were discussed. In the result the Maritime Law Committee was requested to submit a draft code of regulations to a full conference to be held at the Hague in September 1921. A sub-committee was appointed and a code of rules was subsequently adopted under the title of "The Hague Rules, 1921." A full conference of the International Law Association was then convened, at which cargo and shipowning interests were represented by delegates from many nations, and the Hague Rules were passed on the 3rd of September, 1921.

However, whilst the Executive of the Maritime Law Committee was authorised and requested to continue, in conjunction with the representative bodies and interests concerned, to secure the adoption of the Rules, the Rules were not given any mandatory effect, the hope being expressed at that time that the Rules would be generally adopted by shipowners and other carriers of goods by sea and so bring about the desired uniformity in the terms and conditions of contracts of carriage evidenced by bills of lading.

These hopes did not materialise, and whilst a few of the more responsible shipowners gave effect to the Rules in their bills of lading, shipowners generally declined to do so upon the ground that the interests of trade and commerce should be supported by freedom of contract. It was soon apparent that international uniformity in the basic terms of contracts evidenced by bills of lading would not be achieved by voluntary adoption of the Rules and pressure by cargo interests to give the Rules the force of law eventually led to a conference on maritime law being held in Brussels in 1922. As a result of that conference, the Hague Rules, as amended at Brussels in 1923 by a Committee appointed by that conference, were adopted as the basis of a draft convention for the unification of certain rules relating to bills of lading, which was signed at Brussels by delegates from many countries at the International Convention held on the 25th August, 1924.

The United Kingdom was quick to respond, and on the first of January, 1925, the Carriage of Goods by Sea Act, 1924, came into force giving the Rules the force of law in respect of contracts of carriage evidenced by bills of lading covering shipments of goods outwards from the U.K. but excluding coastwise traffic and special shipments covered by non-negotiable receipts. The Commonwealth countries took similar action, eventually being followed by almost all the maritime nations of the world.

THE HAGUE RULES 1924

International Convention for the Unification
of certain Rules of Law relating to
Bills of Lading,
signed at Brussels on 26 August 1924

ARTICLE I

In this Convention the following words are employed with the meanings set out below:

(a) "Carrier" includes the owner or the charterer who enters into a contract of carriage with a shipper.

(b) "Contract of carriage" applies only to contracts of carriage covered by a bill of lading or any similar document of title, in so far as such document relates to the carriage of goods by sea, including any bill of lading or any similar document as aforesaid issued under or pursuant to a charterparty from the moment at which such bill of lading or similar document of title regulates the relations between a carrier and a holder of the same.

(c) "Goods" includes goods, wares, merchandise and articles of every kind whatsoever except live animals and cargo which by the contract of carriage is stated as being carried on deck and is so carried.

(d) "Ship" means any vessel used for the carriage of goods by sea.

(e) "Carriage of goods" covers the period from the time when the goods are loaded on to the time they are discharged from the ship.

ARTICLE II

Subject to the provisions of Article 6, under every contract of carriage of goods by sea the carrier, in relation to the loading, handling, stowage, carriage, custody, care and discharge of such goods, shall be subject to the responsibilities and liabilities, and entitled to the rights and immunities hereinafter set forth.

ARTICLE III

1. The carrier shall be bound before and at the beginning of the voyage to exercise due diligence to:

   (a) Make the ship seaworthy;

   (b) Properly man, equip and supply the ship;

   (c) Make the holds, refrigerating and cool chambers, and all other parts of the ship in which goods are carried, fit and safe for their reception, carriage and preservation.

2. Subject to the provisions of Article 4, the carrier shall properly and carefully load, handle, stow, carry, keep, care for, and discharge the goods carried.

3. After receiving the goods into his charge the carrier or the master or agent of the carrier shall, on demand of the shipper,

issue to the shipper a bill of lading showing among other things:

   (a)   The leading marks necessary for identification of the goods as the same are furnished in writing by the shipper before the loading of such goods starts, provided such marks are stamped or otherwise shown clearly upon the goods if uncovered, or on the cases or coverings in which such goods are contained, in such a manner, as should ordinarily remain legible until the end of the voyage;

   (b)   Either the number of packages or pieces, or the quantity, or weight, as the case may be, as furnished in writing by the shipper;

   (c)   The apparent order and condition of the goods.

Provided that no carrier, master or agent of the carrier shall be bound to state or show in the bill of lading any marks, number, quantity, or weight which he has reasonable ground for suspecting not accurately to represent the goods actually received, or which he has had no reasonable means of checking.

4. Such a bill of lading shall be *prima facie* evidence of the receipt by the carrier of the goods as therein described in accordance with paragraph 3, (a) (b) and (c).

5. The shipper shall be deemed to have guaranteed to the carrier the accuracy at the time of shipment of the marks, number, quantity and weight, as furnished by him, and the shipper shall indemnify the carrier against all loss, damages and expenses arising or resulting from inaccuracies in such particulars. The right of the carrier to such indemnity shall in no way limit his responsibility and liability under the contract of carriage to any person other than the shipper.

6. Unless notice of loss or damage and the general nature of such loss or damage be given in writing to the carrier or his agent at the port of discharge before or at the time of the removal of the goods into the custody of the person entitled to delivery thereof under the contract of carriage, such removal shall be *prima facie* evidence of the delivery by the carrier of the goods as described in the bill of lading.

If the loss or damage is not apparent, the notice must be given within three days of the delivery of the goods.

The notice in writing need not be given if the state of the goods has, at the time of their receipt, been the subject of joint survey or inspection.

In any event the carrier and the ship shall be discharged from all liability in respect of loss or damage unless suit is brought within one year after delivery of the goods or the date when the goods should have been delivered.

In the case of any actual or apprehended loss or damage the carrier and the receiver shall give all reasonable facilities to each other for inspecting and tallying the goods.

7. After the goods are loaded the bill of lading to be issued by the

carrier, master, or agent of the carrier, to the shipper shall, if the shipper so demands, be a "shipped" bill of lading, provided that if the shipper shall have previously taken up any document of title to such goods, he shall surrender the same as against the issue of the "shipped" bill of lading, but at the option of the carrier such document of title may be noted at the port of shipment by the carrier, master, or agent with the name or names of the ship or ships upon which the goods have been shipped and the date or dates of shipment, and when so noted, if it shows the particulars mentioned in paragraph 3 of Article 3, shall for the purpose of this Article be deemed to constitute a "shipped" bill of lading.

8. Any clause, covenant, or agreement in a contract of carriage relieving the carrier or the ship from liability for loss or damage to, or in connexion with, goods arising from negligence, fault, or failure in the duties and obligations provided in this Article or lessening such liability otherwise than as provided in this Convention, shall be null and void and of no effect. A benefit of insurance clause in favour of the carrier or similar clause shall be deemed to be a clause relieving the carrier from liability.

ARTICLE IV

1. Neither the carrier nor the ship shall be liable for loss or damage arising or resulting from unseaworthiness unless caused by want of due diligence on the part of the carrier to make the ship seaworthy, and to secure that the ship is properly manned, equipped and supplied, and to make the holds, refrigerating and cool chambers and all other parts of the ship in which goods are carried fit and safe for their reception, carriage and preservation in accordance with the provisions of paragraph 1 of Article 3. Whenever loss or damage has resulted from unseaworthiness the burden of proving the exercise of due diligence shall be on the carrier or other person claiming exemption under this Article.

2. Neither the carrier nor the ship shall be responsible for loss or damage arising or resulting from:
  - (a) Act, neglect, or default of the master, mariner, pilot, or the servants of the carrier in the navigation or in the management of the ship;
  - (b) Fire, unless caused by the actual fault or privity of the carrier;
  - (c) Perils, dangers and accidents of the sea or other navigable waters;
  - (d) Act of God;
  - (e) Act of war;
  - (f) Act of public enemies;
  - (g) Arrest or restraint of princes, rulers or people, or seizure under legal process;
  - (h) Quarantine restrictions;

(i)   Act or omission of the shipper or owner of the goods, his agent or representative;

(j)   Strikes or lockouts or stoppage or restraint of labour from whatever cause, whether partial or general;

(k)   Riots and civil commotions;

(l)   Saving or attempting to save life or property at sea;

(m)   Wastage in bulk or weight or any other loss or damage arising from inherent defect, quality or vice of the goods;

(n)   Insufficiency of packing;

(o)   Insufficiency or inadequacy of marks;

(p)   Latent defects not discoverable by due diligence;

(q)   Any other cause arising without the actual fault or privity of the carrier, or without the fault or neglect of the agents or servants of the carrier, but the burden of proof shall be on the person claiming the benefit of this exception to show that neither the actual fault or privity of the carrier nor the fault or neglect of the agents or servants of the carrier contributed to the loss or damage.

3. The shipper shall not be responsible for loss or damage sustained by the carrier or the ship arising or resulting from any cause without the act, fault or neglect of the shipper, his agents or his servants.

4. Any deviation in saving or attempting to save life or property at sea or any reasonable deviation shall not be deemed to be an infringement or breach of this Convention or of the contract of carriage, and the carrier shall not be liable for any loss or damage resulting therefrom.

5. Neither the carrier nor the ship shall in any event be or become liable for any loss or damage to or in connexion with goods in an amount exceeding 100 pounds sterling per package or unit, or the equivalent of that sum in other currency unless the nature and value of such goods have been declared by the shipper before shipment and inserted in the bill of lading.

This declaration if embodied in the bill of lading, shall be *prima facie* evidence, but shall not be binding or conclusive on the carrier.

By agreement between the carrier, master or agent of the carrier and the shipper another maximum amount than that mentioned in this paragraph may be fixed, provided that such maximum shall not be less than the figure above named.

Neither the carrier nor the ship shall be responsible in any event for loss or damage to, or in connexion with, goods if the nature or value thereof has been knowingly misstated by the shipper in the bill of lading.

6. Goods of an inflammable, explosive or dangerous nature to the shipment whereof the carrier, master or agent of the carrier has not consented with knowledge of their nature and character, may at any time before discharge be landed at any place, or

destroyed or rendered innocuous by the carrier without compensation and the shipper of such goods shall be liable for all damages and expenses directly or indirectly arising out of or resulting from such shipment. If any such goods shipped with such knowledge and consent shall become a danger to the ship or cargo, they may in like manner be landed at any place, or destroyed or rendered innocuous by the carrier without liability on the part of the carrier except to general average, if any.

ARTICLE V

A carrier shall be at liberty to surrender in whole or in part all or any of his rights and immunities or to increase any of his responsibilities and obligations under this Convention, provided such surrender or increase shall be embodied in the bill of lading issued to the shipper.

The provisions of this Convention shall not be applicable to charterparties, but if bills of lading are issued in the case of a ship under a charterparty they shall comply with the terms of this Convention. Nothing in these rules shall be held to prevent the insertion in a bill of lading of any lawful provision regarding general average.

ARTICLE VI

Notwithstanding the provisions of the preceding Articles, a carrier, master or agent of the carrier and a shipper shall in regard to any particular goods be at liberty to enter into any agreement in any terms as to the responsibility and liability of the carrier for such goods, and as to the rights and immunities of the carrier in respect of such goods, or his obligation as to seaworthiness, so far as this stipulation is not contrary to public policy, or the care or diligence of his servants or agents in regard to the loading, handling, stowage, carriage, custody, care and discharge of the goods carried by sea, provided that in this case no bill of lading has been or shall be issued and that the terms agreed shall be embodied in a receipt which shall be a non-negotiable document and shall be marked as such.

Any agreement so entered into shall have full legal effect.

Provided that this Article shall not apply to ordinary commercial shipments made in the ordinary course of trade, but only to other shipments where the character or condition of the property to be carried or the circumstances, terms and conditions under which the carriage is to be performed are such as reasonably to justify a special agreement.

ARTICLE VII

Nothing herein contained shall prevent a carrier or a shipper from entering into any agreement, stipulation, condition, reservation or exemption as to the responsibility and liability of the carrier or the ship for the loss or damage to, or in connexion with, the custody and care and handling of goods prior to the loading on, and subsequent to, the discharge from the ship on which the goods are carried by sea.

ARTICLE VIII

The provisions of this Convention shall not affect the rights and obligations of the carrier under any statute for the time being in force relating to the limitation of the liability of owners of seagoing vessels.

ARTICLE IX

The monetary units mentioned in this Convention are to be taken to be gold value.

Those contracting States in which the pound sterling is not a monetary unit reserve to themselves the right of translating the sums indicated in this Convention in terms of pound sterling into terms of their own monetary system in round figures.

The national laws may reserve to the debtor the right of discharging his debt in national currency according to the rate of exchange prevailing on the day of the arrival of the ship at the port of discharge of the goods concerned.

ARTICLE X

The provisions of this Convention shall apply to all bills of lading issued in any of the contracting States.

ARTICLE XI

After an interval of not more than two years from the day on which the Convention is signed the Belgian Government shall place itself in communication with the Governments of the High Contracting Parties which have declared themselves prepared to ratify the Convention, with a view to deciding whether it shall be put into force. The ratifications shall be deposited at Brussels at a date to be fixed by agreement among the said Governments. The first deposit of ratifications shall be recorded in a procés-verbal signed by the representatives of the Powers which take part therein and by the Belgian Minister for Foreign Affairs.

The subsequent deposit of ratifications shall be made by means of a written notification, addressed to the Belgian Government and accompanied by the instrument of ratification.

A duly certified copy of the procés-verbal relating to the first deposit of ratifications, of the notifications referred to in the previous paragraph, and also of the instruments of ratification accompanying them, shall be immediately sent by the Belgian Government through the diplomatic channel to the Powers who have signed this Convention or who have acceded to it. In the cases contemplated in the preceding paragraph, the said Government shall inform them at the same time of the date on which it received the notification.

ARTICLE XII

Non-signatory States may accede to the present Convention whether or not they have been represented at the International Conference at Brussels.

A State which desires to accede shall notify its intention in writing to the Belgian Government, forwarding to it the document of accession, which shall be deposited in the archives of the said Government.

The Belgian Government shall immediately forward to all the States which have signed or acceded to the Convention a duly certified copy of the notification and of the act of accession, mentioning the date on which it received the notification.

ARTICLE XIII

The High Contracting Parties may at the time of signature, ratification or accession declare that their acceptance of the present Convention does not include any or all of the self-governing dominions, or of the colonies, overseas possessions, protectorates or territories under their sovereignty or authority, and they may subsequently accede separately on behalf of any self-governing dominion, colony, overseas possession, protectorate or territory excluded in their declaration. They may also denounce the Convention separately in accordance with its provisions in respect of any self-governing dominion, or any colony, overseas possession, protectorate or territory under their sovereignty or authority.

ARTICLE XIV

The present Convention shall take effect, in the case of the States which have taken part in the first deposit of ratifications, one year after the date of the protocol recording such deposit.

As respects the States which ratify subsequently or which accede, and also in cases in which the Convention is subsequently put into effect in accordance with Article 13, it shall take effect six months after the notifications specified in paragraph 2 of Article 11 and paragraph 2 of Article 12 have been received by the Belgian Government.

ARTICLE XV

In the event of one of the contracting States wishing to denounce the present Convention, the denunciation shall be notified in writing to the Belgian Government, which shall immediately communicate a duly certified copy of the notification to all the other States, informing them of the date on which it was received.

The denunciation shall only operate in respect of the State which made the notification, and on the expiry of one year after the notification has reached the Belgian Government.

ARTICLE XVI

Any one of the contracting States shall have the right to call for a fresh conference with a view to considering possible amendments.

A State which would exercise this right should notify its intention to the other States through the Belgian Government, which would make arrangements for convening the conference.

Done at Brussels, in a single copy, August 25th, 1924.

(Follow the signatures)

PROTOCOL OF SIGNATURE

At the time of signing the International Convention for the unification of certain rules of law relating to bills of lading the Plenipotentiaries whose signatures appear below have adopted this Protocol, which will have the same force and the same value as if its provisions were inserted in the text of the Convention to which it relates.

The High Contracting Parties may give effect to this Convention either by giving it the force of law or by including in their national legislation in a form appropriate to that legislation the rules adopted under this Convention.

They may reserve the right:

1.   To prescribe that in the cases referred to in paragraph 2 (c) to (p) of Article 4 the holder of a bill of lading shall be entitled to establish responsibility for loss or damage arising from the personal fault of the carrier or the fault of his servants which are not covered by paragraph (a).

2. To apply Article 6 in so far as the national coasting trade is concerned to all classes of goods without taking account of the restriction set out in the last paragraph of that Article.

Done at Brussels, in a single copy, August 25th, 1924.

(Follow the signatures)

Events leading to the Visby Rules as agreed at the Stockholm Conference of the Comite Maritime International in June, 1963.

It was, of course, a natural sequence of events that shipowners and cargo interests should test the effect of the Hague Rules, particularly in the light of the flood of claims put forward by cargo underwriters and cargo interests generally which followed upon the Rules being given the effect of law in the United Kingdom in January 1925 by the passing of the Carriage of Goods by Sea Act, 1924.

From time to time the courts would be called upon to decide how and in what manner a particular provision or provisions of the Rules should be construed and applied, in order to settle disputes between cargo and shipowning interests on the question of liability in respect of cargo loss or damage. And over the next three to four decades, as a result of these test cases brought before the courts, shipowning and cargo interests became aware of their respective positions under the Rules.

Among the more important decisions by the Courts there was the ruling that stevedores were to be regarded as servants of the shipowner thereby making the carrier liable for cargo loss or damage caused by such parties during the period of the application of the Rules to the bill of lading contract. The exception contained in the Rules that neither the carrier nor the ship shall become liable for cargo loss or damage arising out of neglect in the navigation or management of the ship, received the attention of the courts clarifying the difference between care of cargo and care of ship. The duty of the carrier under the Rules to exercise due diligence to make the ship seaworthy was another bone of contention between shipowning and cargo interests which was constantly before the courts to enable the parties to understand their respective positions under the Rules.

Generally speaking these law cases have so clarified the effect of the Hague Rules as signed at the Conference in Brussels in August, 1924, that it is now rare that commercial men are in any doubt or dispute (over cargo loss or damage) as to the party who must bear the burden of such loss. However, as the years progressed it became apparent that certain amendments to the Rules could be made, for example a review of the limits of the carrier's liability. Sparked into life by a ruling in the House of Lords, there was a review of the issue of unseaworthiness, which led to an amendment to the Rules being put forward in the Visby Rules at the Stockholm Conference of the Comite Maritime International in June 1963.

The case before the House of Lords (*The Muncaster Castle*) concerned cargo damage arising out of the negligent failure of a ship repair yard's fitter properly to harden up the nuts on the inspection covers of the storm valves, so allowing the entry of seawater into the hold of the vessel on a subsequent voyage. The House of Lords overruled the ruling of the trial court and the Court of Appeal and held that the shipowners were liable for the damage done to the cargo. And in so holding the court said that the words "exercise of due diligence to make the ship seaworthy" in the Hague Rules were adopted from the American Harter Act, 1893, and similar British Commonwealth Statutes, and that those words should be given the meaning attributed to them prior to the Hague Rules. It followed that, accordingly, a carrier was responsible to the cargo owner unless due diligence in the work had been shown by every person to whom any part of the necessary work had been entrusted, no matter whether he was the carrier's servant, agent or independent contractor, and that, therefore, the shipowners were liable for the negligence of the ship repair yard's fitter.

However, there was great opposition to the proposed amendment (contained in Article 1 paragraph 1 of the Visby Rules) on the issue of unseaworthiness, so much so that the adoption of all the other Visby Rules was delayed, and, in the end, the proposed amendment was redrafted but was dropped at the time of the Brussels Protocol, 1968.

Other amendments contained in Article 1 included two changes of the Hague Rules relating to time limitation for the commencement of suit which were introduced with the object of clarifying the Hague Rules in this respect. These are contained in Article 1 paragraph 3. An additional provision relative to recourse actions was added to the Hague Rules, this being contained in Article 1 paragraph 4. The monetary limitation contained in the Hague Rules was amended, the amendments being contained in Article 2.

The effect of the successful action brought by a passenger in the steamship *Himalaya* against the master and bosun of the vessel, leading to the drafting of the "Himalaya" clause to give the servants or agents of the carrier the same benefits of exemptions from and limitations of liability contained in the bill of lading and the Hague Rules, will be well remembered. Article 3 of the Visby Rules contains a special provision to be added to the Hague Rules which amongst other things, would, in the event of an action against a servant or agent of the carrier (such servant or agent not being an independent contractor), give such persons the right to avail themselves of the defences and limits of liability which the carrier would be entitled to invoke under the Hague Rules.

Article 5 of the Visby Rules provided for the deletion of Article 10 of the Hague Rules to be replaced by a provision which was aimed at making the Hague Rules mandatory throughout the world. This provision was varied at the Brussels Convention in 1967/1968 when the Brussels Protocol 1968 was agreed.

The Stockholm Conference in 1963, when the Visby Rules were introduced, was the result of a review of the legal events and actions arising over the three to four decades following upon the introduction of the Hague Rules in 1924. The Rules were the result of very careful thought on the part of the delegates to that conference as to the manner in which they should be amended to bring them up to date with current thinking. And eventually, either in whole or in part, they came to be included in the Brussels Protocol of 1968, that is with the outstanding exception of the proposed alteration arising out of the ruling of the House of Lords in the case of the *Muncaster Castle*.

VISBY RULES

Protocol or International Convention to Amend the International Convention for the Unification of Certain Rules of Law relating to Bills of Lading Signed in Brussels on the 25th August, 1924, adopted at the Stockholm Conference of the Comité Maritime International in June 1963.

ARTICLE I

§1. In Article 3, §1 of the 1924 Convention shall be added:
"Provided that if in circumstances in which it is proper to employ an independent contractor (including a Classification Society), the Carrier has taken care to appoint one of repute as regards competence, the Carrier shall not be deemed to have failed to exercise due diligence solely by reason of an act or omission on the part of such an independent contractor, his servants or agents (including any independent sub-contractor and his servants or agents) in respect of the construction, repair or maintenance of the ship or any part thereof or of her equipment. Nothing contained in this proviso shall absolve the Carrier from taking such precautions by way of supervision or inspection as may be reasonable in relation to any work carried out by such an independent contractor as aforesaid."

§2. In Article 3, §4 shall be added:
"However, proof to the contrary shall not be admissible when the Bill of Lading has been transferred to a third party acting in good faith."

§3. In Article 3, §6, paragraph 4 is deleted and replaced by:
"In any event the carrier and the ship shall be discharged from all liability whatsoever in respect of the goods unless suit is brought within one year after delivery of the goods or the date when the goods should have been delivered. Such a period may, however, be extended should the parties concerned so agree."

§4. In Article 3, after paragraph 6 shall be added the following paragraph 6 bis:
"Recourse actions may be brought even after the expiration of the year provided for in the preceding paragraph if brought within the time allowed by the law of the Court seized of the case. However, the time allowed shall be not less than three months, commencing from day when the person bringing such recourse action has settled the claim or has been served with process in the action against himself."

ARTICLE II

§1. In Article 4 of the Convention the first sub-paragraph of paragraph 5 is deleted and replaced by the following:

"Neither the carrier nor the ship shall in any event be or become liable for any loss or damage to or in connection with the goods in an amount exceeding the equivalent of 10,000 francs per package or unit, each franc consisting of 65,5 milligrams of gold of millesimal fineness 900, unless the nature and value of such goods have been declared by the shipper before shipment and inserted in the Bill of Lading."

§2. In Article 4, paragraph 5 shall be added the following:
"The date of conversion of the sum awarded into national currencies shall be regulated in accordance with the law of the court seized of the case."

§3. Article 9 of the Convention is deleted.

ARTICLE III

Between Articles 4 and 5 of the Convention shall be inserted the following Article 4 bis:

"1. The defences and limits of liability provided for in this Convention shall apply in any action against the carrier in respect of loss or damage to goods covered by a contract of carriage whether the action be founded in contract or in tort.

2. If such an action is brought against a servant or agent of the carrier (such servant or agent not being an independent contractor), such servant or agent shall be entitled to avail himself of the defences and limits of liability which the carrier is entitled to invoke under this Convention.

3. The aggregate of the amounts recoverable from the carrier, and such servants and agents, shall in no case exceed the limit provided for in this Convention."

ARTICLE IV

Article 9 of the Convention shall be deleted and replaced by the following:

"This Convention shall not affect the provisions of any international Convention or national law which governs liability for nuclear damage."

ARTICLE V

Article 10 of the Convention is deleted and replaced by the following:

"The provisions of this Convention shall apply to every bill of lading for carriage of goods from one State to another, under which bill of lading the port of loading, of discharge or one of the optional ports of discharge, is situated in a Contracting State, whatever may be the law governing such bill of lading and whatever may be the nationality of the ship, the carrier, the shipper, the consignee or any other interested person."

Events leading to the Brussels Protocol 1968 signed at Brussels in February 1968 following the 1967-1968 session of the Diplomatic Conference on Maritime Law.

AGREEMENT over the Visby Rules was delayed because of the tremendous controversy that developed arising out of the proposed amendment to the Hague Rules brought about by the House of Lords' decision in the *Muncaster Castle* case.

Meanwhile, a new development in the transportation of goods over sea and over land was beginning to materialise, a development that was not (or, it might be said, *could* not have been) foreseen at the time of the introduction of the Hague Rules in 1924, namely the transportation of goods in containers. Questions were arising as to whether such containers constituted a "package or unit" within the meaning of the Hague Rules and whether the carrier of goods transported in those containers was entitled to apply the Hague Rules limitation of liability "per package" to the container. In other words did the container constitute a "package or unit" within the meaning of the Hague Rules.

The issue was of extreme importance to both cargo and shipping interests, in that a cargo owner would be entitled to recover from the shipowner for loss or damage to his goods, up to the limitation provided in the Hague Rules, in respect of each of the packages shipped. But if those packages had been packed in a container the shipowner would argue that the container constituted the package, and so apply the Hague Rules limitation of liability to the container. It was fast becoming apparent, particularly in the light of the development of the container ship, that the provisions of the Hague Rules as regards limitation of liability should be urgently reviewed, particularly in the light of the fact that a coventional dry cargo ship might be carrying goods packed in containers for different consignees, and at the same time be carrying goods packed in a conventional manner. On the one hand, if the shipowners' construction of the Hague Rules was to prevail, the shipowner would need to accept liability for loss of or damage to the goods packed conventionally "per package" whereas the consignees of goods shipped in containers would only be able to recover proportionately the limitation of liability. Clearly the position needed to be clarified, this being one of the events leading to the Brussels Protocol, 1968.

It also became clear that other matters which were the subject of the Visby Rules needed to be reviewed and, in the outcome, the Visby Rules were re-drafted, in their present form, for international adoption. So far as the United Kingdom is concerned, the amendments agreed at the Convention are incorporated in the Carriage of Goods by Sea Act, 1971.

Article 1 paragraph 1 of the 1968 Brussels Protocol amends Article 111 paragraph 4 of the Rules. Article 1 paragraph 2 of the Protocol has reference to time limitation for the commencement of suit and replaces Article 111 paragraph 6 sub paragraph 4 of the Hague Rules with a new provision clarifying the Hague Rules in this respect. Article 1 paragraph 3 of the Protocol again refers to time limitation and provides for a new paragraph to be contained in the Hague Rules to follow Article 111 paragraph 6 of the Rules.

Article 2 of the Protocol makes sweeping changes as regards the monetary limitation provisions of the Hague Rules, replacing Article IV, paragraph 5 of the Rules completely, and dealing also with the container problem. Article 3 of the Protocol provides for the insertion of a new paragraph between Articles IV and V of the Hague Rules which provides, amongst other things, for the defences and limits of liability contained in the Hague Rules to be available to the servants or agents of the carrier. Article 4 of the Protocol replaces Article IX of the Hague Rules (which relates to monetary units in the Hague Rules no longer applicable because of the amendments) with a provision governing liability for nuclear damage. Article 5 of the Protocol replaces Article X of the Hague Rules, which governs the applicability of the Rules to contracting States, with new provisions amending also the provisions of the Visby Rules in this respect.

Under its provisions, the Protocol was to come into force three months after ratification or accession by ten States, of which at least five had to have over 1,000,000 gross tons of shipping. In 1977 sufficient countries had ratified the Protocol and it came into force on the 23rd June, 1977.

THE 1968 BRUSSELS PROTOCOL

Protocol to amend the International Convention for the unification of certain rules of law relating to bills of lading, signed at Brussels 23rd of February 1968

THE CONTRACTING PARTIES

Considering that it is desirable to amend the International Convention for the unification of certain rules of law relating to bills of lading, signed at Brussels on 25 August 1924,

Have agreed as follows:

Article 1. 1. In Article 3, paragraph 4 shall be added:

"However, proof to the contrary shall not be admissible when the Bill of Lading has been transferred to a third party acting in good faith."

2. In Article 3, paragraph 6, sub-paragraph 4 shall be replaced by:

"Subject to paragraph 6 *bis* the carrier and the ship shall in any event be discharged from all liability whatsoever in respect of the goods, unless suit is brought within one year of their delivery or of the date when they should have been delivered. This period may, however, be extended if the parties so agree after the cause of action has arisen."

3. In Article 3, after paragraph 6 shall be added the following paragraph 6 *bis*:

"An action for indemnity against a third person may be brought even after the expiration of the year provided for in the preceding paragraph if brought within the time allowed by the law of the Court seized of the case. However, the time allowed shall be not less than three months, commencing from the day when the person bringing such action for indemnity has settled the claim or has been served with process in the action against himself."

Article 2. Article 4, paragraph 5 shall be deleted and replaced by the following:

(a) Unless the nature and value of such goods have been declared by the shipper before shipment and inserted in the Bill of Lading, neither the carrier nor the ship shall in any event be or become liable for any loss or damage to or in connexion with the goods in an amount exceeding the equivalent of Frcs. 10,000 per package or unit or Frcs. 30 per kilo of gross weight of the goods lost or damaged, whichever is the higher.

(b) The total amount recoverable shall be calculated by reference to the value of such goods at the place and time at which the goods are discharged from the ship in accordance with the contract or should have been so discharged.

The value of the goods shall be fixed according to the commodity exchange price, or, if there be no such price, according to the current market price, or, if there be no commodity exchange price or current market price, by reference to the normal value of goods of the same kind and quality. ·

(c) Where a container, pallet or similar article of transport is used to consolidate goods, the number of packages or units enumerated in the Bill of Lading as packed in such article of transport shall be deemed the number of packages or units for the purpose of this paragraph as far as these packages or units are concerned, except as aforesaid such article of transport shall be considered the package or unit.

(d) A franc means a unit consisting of 65.5 milligrammes of gold of millesimal fineness 900'. The date of conversion of the sum awarded into national currencies shall be governed by the law of the Court seized of the case.

(e) Neither the carrier nor the ship shall be entitled to the benefit of the limitation of liability provided for in this paragraph if it is proved that the damage resulted from an act or omission of the carrier done with intent to cause damage, or recklessly and with knowledge that damage would probably result.

(f) The declaration mentioned in sub-paragraph (a) of this paragraph, if embodied in the bill of lading, shall be *prima facie* evidence, but shall not be binding or conclusive on the carrier.

(g) By agreement between the carrier, master or agent of the carrier and the shipper other maximum amounts than those mentioned in sub-paragraph (a) of this paragraph may be fixed, provided that no maximum amount so fixed shall be less than the appropriate maximum mentioned in that sub-paragraph.

(h) Neither the carrier nor the ship shall be responsible in any event for loss or damage to, or in connexion with, goods if the nature or value thereof has been knowingly misstated by the shipper in the bill of lading.

Article 3. Between Articles 4 and 5 of the Convention shall be inserted the following Article 4 *bis:*

1. The defences and limits of liability provided for in this Convention shall apply in any action against the carrier in respect of loss or damage to goods covered by a contract of carriage whether the action be founded in contract or in tort.

2. If such an action is brought against a servant or agent of the carrier (such servant or agent not being an independent contractor), such servant or agent shall be entitled to avail himself of the defences and limits of liability which the carrier is entitled to invoke under this Convention.

3. The aggregate of the amounts recoverable from the carrier, and such servants and agents, shall in no case exceed the limit provided for in this Convention.

4. Nevertheless, a servant or agent of the carrier shall not be entitled to avail himself of the provisions of this Article, if it is proved that the damage resulted from an act or omission of the servant or agent done with intent to cause damage or recklessly and with knowledge that damage would probably result.

Article 4. Article 9 of the Convention shall be replaced by the following:

"This Convention shall not affect the provisions of any international Convention or national law governing liability for nuclear damage".

Article 5. Article 10 of the Convention shall be replaced by the following:

"The provisions of this Convention shall apply to every Bill of Lading relating to the carriage of goods between ports in two different States if:

(a) the Bill of Lading is issued in a contracting State,
    or

(b) the carriage is from a port in a contracting State,

or

(c) the Contract contained in or evidenced by the Bill of Lading provides that the rules of this Convention or legislation of any State giving effect to them are to govern the contract whatever may be the nationality of the ship, the carrier, the shipper, the consignee, or any other interested person.

Each contracting State shall apply the provisions of this Convention to the Bills of Lading mentioned above.

This Article shall not prevent a Contracting State from applying the Rules of this Convention to Bills of Lading not included in the preceding paragraphs".

Article 6. As between the Parties to this Protocol the Convention and the Protocol shall be read and interpreted together as one single instrument.

A Party to this Protocol shall have no duty to apply the provisions of this Protocol to bills of lading issued in a State which is a Party to the Convention but which is not a Party to this Protocol.

Article 7. As between the Parties to this Protocol, denunciation by any of them of the Convention in accordance with Article 15 thereof, shall not be construed in any way as a denunciation of the Convention as amended by this Protocol.

Article 8. Any dispute between two or more Contracting Parties concerning the interpretation or application of the Convention which cannot be settled through negotiation shall, at the request of one of them, be submitted to arbitration. If within six months from the date of the request for arbitration the Parties are unable to agree on the organization of the arbitration, any one of those Parties may refer the dispute to the International Court of Justice by request in conformity with the Statute of the Court.

Article 9. 1. Each Contracting Party may at the time of signature or ratification of this Protocol or accession thereto, declare that it does not consider itself bound by Article 8 of this Protocol. The other Contracting Parties shall not be bound by this Article with respect of any Contracting Party having made such a reservation.

2. Any Contracting Party having made a reservation in accordance with paragraph 1 may at any time withdraw this reservation by notification to the Belgian Government.

Article 10. This Protocol shall be open for signature by the States which have ratified the Convention or which have adhered thereto before 23 February 1968, and by any State represented at the twelfth session (1967-1968) of the Diplomatic Conference on Maritime Law.

Article 11. 1. This Protocol shall be ratified:

2. Ratification of this Protocol by any State which is not a

Party to the Convention shall have the effect of accession to the Convention.

3. The instruments of ratification shall be deposited with the Belgian Government.

Article 12. 1. States, Members of the United Nations or Members of the specialized agencies of the United Nations, not represented at the twelfth session of the Diplomatic Conference on Maritime Law, may accede to this Protocol.

2. Accession to this Protocol shall have the effect of accession to the Convention.

3. The instruments of accession shall be deposited with the Belgian Government.

Article 13. 1. This Protocol shall come into force three months after the date of the deposit of ten instruments of ratification or accession, of which at least five shall have been deposited by States that have each a tonnage equal or superior to one million gross tons of tonnage.

2. For each State which ratifies this Protocol or accede thereto after the date of deposit of the instrument of ratification or accession determining the coming into force such as is stipulated in paragraph 1 of this Article, this Protocol shall come into force three months after the deposit of its instrument of ratification or accession.

Article 14. 1. Any Contracting State may denounce this Protocol by notification to the Belgian Government.

2. This denunciation shall have the effect of denunciation of the Convention.

3. The denunciation shall take effect one year after the date on which the notification has been received by the Belgian Government.

Article 15. 1. Any Contracting State may at the time of signature, ratification or accession

or at any time thereafter declare by written notification to the Belgian Government which among the territories under its sovereignty or for whose international relations it is responsible, are those to which the present Protocol applies.

The Protocol shall three months after the date of the receipt of such notification by the Belgian Government extend to the territories named therein, but not before the date of the coming into force of the Protocol in respect of such State.

2. This extension also shall apply to the Convention if the latter is not yet applicable to those territories.

3. Any Contracting State which has made a declaration under paragraph 1 of this Article may at any time thereafter declare by notification given to the Belgian Government that the Protocol shall cease to extend to such territory. This denunciation shall take effect one year after the date on which notification thereof has been received by the Belgian Government; it also shall apply

to the Convention.

Article 16. The Contracting Parties may give effect to this Protocol either by giving it the force of law or by including in their national legislation in a form appropriate to that legislation the rules adopted under this Protocol.

Article 17. The Belgian Government shall notify the States represented at the twelfth session (1967-1968) of the Diplomatic Conference on Maritime Law, the acceding States to this Protocol, and the States Parties to the Convention, of the following:

1. The signatures, ratifications and accessions received in accordance with Articles 10, 11 and 12.

2. The date on which the present Protocol will come into force in accordance with Article 13.

3. The notifications with regard to the territorial application in accordance with Article 15.

4. The denunciations received in accordance with Article 14.

IN WITNESS WHEREOF the undersigned Plenipotentiaries, duly authorized, have signed this Protocol.

DONE at Brussels, this 23rd day of February 1968, in the French and English languages, both texts being equally authentic, in a single copy, which shall remain deposited in the archives of the Belgian Government, which shall issue certified copies.

HAGUE-VISBY RULES

*The Hague Rules as Amended by the Brussels
Protocol 1968*

ARTICLE 1

In these Rules the following words are employed, with the
meanings set out below:

(a) "Carrier" includes the owner or the charterer who enters
into a contract of carriage with a shipper.

(b) "Contract of carriage" applies only to contracts of
carriage covered by a bill of lading or any similar
document of title, in so far as such document relates to the
carriage of goods by sea, including any bill of lading or
any similar document as aforesaid issued under or pursuant to a charter party from the moment at which such
bill of lading or similar document of title regulates the
relations between a carrier and a holder of the same.

(c) "Goods" includes goods, wares, merchandise, and
articles of every kind whatsoever except live animals and
cargo which by the contract of carriage is stated as being
carried on deck and is so carried.

(d) "Ship" means any vessel used for the carriage of goods by
sea.

(e) "Carriage of goods" covers the period from the time
when the goods are loaded on to the time they are discharged from the ship.

ARTICLE II

Subject to the provisions of Article VI, under every contract of
carriage of goods by sea the carrier, in relation to the loading,
handling, stowage, carriage, custody, care and discharge of such
goods, shall be subject to the responsibilities and liabilities, and
entitled to the rights and immunities hereinafter set forth.

ARTICLE III

1. The carrier shall be bound before and at the beginning of the
voyage to exercise due diligence to:

(a) Make the ship seaworthy.

(b) Properly man, equip and supply the ship.

(c) Make the holds, refrigerating and cool chambers, and all
other parts of the ship in which goods are carried, fit and
safe for their reception, carriage and preservation.

2. Subject to the provisions of Article IV, the carrier shall
properly and carefully load, handle, stow, carry, keep, care for,
and discharge the goods carried.

3. After receiving the goods into his charge the carrier or the master or agent of the carrier shall, on demand of the shipper, issue to the shipper a bill of lading showing among other things:

(a) The leading marks necessary for identification of the goods as the same are furnished in writing by the shipper before the loading of such goods starts, provided such marks are stamped or otherwise shown clearly upon the goods if uncovered, or on the cases or coverings in which such goods are contained, in such a manner as should ordinarily remain legible until the end of the voyage.

(b) Either the number of packages or pieces, or the quantity, or weight, as the case may be, as furnished in writing by the shipper.

(c) The apparent order and condition of the goods.

Provided that no carrier, master or agent of the carrier shall be bound to state or show in the bill of lading any marks, number, quantity, or weight which he has reasonable ground for suspecting not accurately to represent the goods actually received, or which he has had no reasonable means of checking.

4. Such a bill of lading shall be primâ facie evidence of the receipt by the carrier of the goods as therein described in accordance with paragraph 3 (a), (b) and (c). However, proof to the contrary shall not be admissible when the bill of lading has been transferred to a third party acting in good faith.

5. The shipper shall be deemed to have guaranteed to the carrier the accuracy at the time of shipment of the marks, number, quantity and weight, as furnished by him, and the shipper shall indemnify the carrier against all loss, damages and expenses arising or resulting from inaccuracies in such particulars. The right of the carrier to such indemnity shall in no way limit his responsibility and liability under the contract of carriage to any person other than the shipper.

6. Unless notice of loss or damage and the general nature of such loss or damage be given in writing to the carrier or his agent at the port of discharge before or at the time of the removal of the goods into the custody of the person entitled to delivery thereof under the contract of carriage, or, if the loss or damage be not apparent, within three days, such removal shall be primâ facie evidence of the delivery by the carrier of the goods as described in the bill of lading.

The notice in writing need not be given if the state of the goods has, at the time of their receipt, been the subject of joint survey or inspection.

Subject to paragraph 6bis the carrier and the ship shall in any event be discharged from all liability whatsoever in respect of the goods, unless suit is brought within one year of their delivery or of the date when they should have been delivered. This period may, however, be extended if the parties so agree after the cause of action has arisen.

In the case of any actual or apprehended loss or damage the carrier and the receiver shall give all reasonable facilities to each other for inspecting and tallying the goods.

6bis. An action for indemnity against a third person may be brought even after the expiration of the year provided for in the preceding paragraph if brought within the time allowed by the law of the Court seized of the case. However, the time allowed shall be not less than three months, commencing from the day when the person bringing such action for indemnity has settled the claim or has been served with process in the action against himself.

7. After the goods are loaded the bill of lading to be issued by the carrier, master, or agent of the carrier, to the shipper shall, if the shipper so demands, be a "shipped" bill of lading, provided that if the shipper shall have previously taken up any document of title to such goods, he shall surrender the same as against the issue of the "shipped" bill of lading, but at the option of the carrier such document of title may be noted at the port of shipment by the carrier, master, or agent with the name or names of the ship or ships upon which the goods have been shipped and the date or dates of shipment, and when so noted, if it shows the particulars mentioned in paragraph 3 of Article III, shall for the purpose of this article be deemed to constitute a "shipped" bill of lading.

8. Any clause, covenant, or agreement in a contract of carriage relieving the carrier or the ship from liability for loss or damage to, or in connection with, goods arising from negligence, fault, or failure in the duties and obligations provided in this article or lessening such liability otherwise than as provided in these Rules, shall be null and void and of no effect. A benefit of insurance in favour of the carrier or similar clause shall be deemed to be a clause relieving the carrier from liability.

ARTICLE IV

1. Neither the carrier nor the ship shall be liable for loss or damage arising or resulting from unseaworthiness unless caused by want of due diligence on the part of the carrier to make the ship seaworthy, and to secure that the ship is properly manned, equipped and supplied, and to make the holds, refrigerating and cool chambers and all other parts of the ship in which goods are carried fit and safe for their reception, carriage and preservation in accordance with the provisions of paragraph 1 of Article III. Whenever loss or damage has resulted from unseaworthiness the burden of proving the exercise of due diligence shall be on the carrier or other person claiming exemption under this article.

2. Neither the carrier nor the ship shall be responsible for loss or damage arising or resulting from:

(a) Act, neglect, or default of the master, mariner, pilot, or the servants of the carrier in the navigation or in the management of the ship.

(b) Fire, unless caused by the actual fault or privity of the carrier.

(c) Perils, dangers and accidents of the sea or other navigable waters.

(d) Act of God.

(e) Act of war.

(f) Act of public enemies.

(g) Arrest or restraint of princes, rulers or people, or seizure under legal process.

(h) Quarantine restrictions.

(i) Act or omission of the shipper or owner of the goods, his agent or representative.

(j) Strikes or lockouts or stoppage or restraint of labour from whatever cause, whether partial or general.

(k) Riots and civil commotions.

(l) Saving or attempting to save life or property at sea.

(m) Wastage in bulk or weight or any other loss or damage arising from inherent defect, quality or vice of the goods.

(n) Insufficiency of packing.

(o) Insufficiency or inadequacy of marks.

(p) Latent defects not discoverable by due diligence.

(q) Any other cause arising without the actual fault or privity of the carrier, or without the fault or neglect of the agents or servants of the carrier, but the burden of proof shall be on the person claiming the benefit of this exception to show that neither the actual fault or privity of the carrier nor the fault or neglect of the agents or servants of the carrier contributed to the loss or damage.

3. The shipper shall not be responsible for loss or damage sustained by the carrier or the ship arising or resulting from any cause without the act, fault or neglect of the shipper, his agents or his servants.

4. Any deviation in saving or attempting to save life or property at sea or any reasonable deviation shall not be deemed to be an infringement or breach of these Rules or of the contract of carriage, and the carrier shall not be liable for any loss or damage resulting therefrom.

5. (a) Unless the nature and value of such goods have been declared by the shipper before shipment and inserted in the bill of lading, neither the carrier nor the ship shall in any event be or become liable for any loss or damage to or in connection with the goods in an amount exceeding the equivalent of 10,000 francs per package or unit or 30 francs per kilo of gross weight of the goods lost or damaged, whichever is the higher.

(*b*) The total amount recoverable shall be calculated by reference to the value of such goods at the place and time at which the goods are discharged from the ship in accordance with the contract or should have been so discharged.

The value of the goods shall be fixed according to the commodity exchange price, or, if there be no such price, according to the current market price, or, if there be no commodity exchange price or current market price, by reference to the normal value of goods of the same kind and quality.

(*c*) Where a container, pallet or similar article of transport is used to consolidate goods, the number of packages or units enumerated in the bill of lading as packed in such article of transport shall be deemed the number of packages or units for the purpose of this paragraph as far as these packages or units are concerned. Except as aforesaid such article of transport shall be considered the package or unit.

(*d*) A franc means a unit consisting of 65.5 milligrammes of gold of millesimal fineness 900. The date of conversion of the sum awarded into national currencies shall be governed by the law of the Court seized of the case.

(*e*) Neither the carrier nor the ship shall be entitled to the benefit of the limitation of liability provided for in this paragraph if it is proved that the damage resulted from an act or omission of the carrier done with intent to cause damage, or recklessly and with knowledge that damage would probably result.

(*f*) The declaration mentioned in sub-paragraph (*a*) of this paragraph, if embodied in the bill of lading, shall be prima facie evidence, but shall not be binding or conclusive on the carrier.

(*g*) By agreement between the carrier, master or agent of the carrier and the shipper other maximum amounts than those mentioned in sub-paragraph (*a*) of this paragraph may be fixed, provided that no maximum amount so fixed shall be less than the appropriate maximum mentioned in that sub-paragraph.

(*h*) Neither the carrier nor the ship shall be responsible in any event for loss or damage to, or in connection with, goods if the nature or value thereof has been knowingly mis-stated by the shipper in the bill of lading.

6. Goods of an inflammable, explosive or dangerous nature to the shipment whereof the carrier, master or agent of the carrier has not consented with knowledge of their nature and character, may at any time before discharge be landed at any place, or destroyed or rendered innocuous by the carrier without compensation and the shipper of such goods shall be liable for all damages and expenses directly or indirectly arising out of or resulting from such shipment. If any such goods shipped with such knowledge and consent shall become a danger to the ship or cargo, they may in like manner be landed at any place, or

destroyed or rendered innocuous by the carrier without liability on the part of the carrier except to general average, if any.

ARTICLE IV BIS

1. The defences and limits of liability provided for in these Rules shall apply in any action against the carrier in respect of loss or damage to goods covered by a contract of carriage whether the action be founded in contract or in tort.

2. If such an action is brought against a servant or agent of the carrier (such servant or agent not being an independent contractor), such servant or agent shall be entitled to avail himself of the defences and limits of liability which the carrier is entitled to invoke under these Rules.

3. The aggregate of the amounts recoverable from the carrier, and such servants and agents, shall in no case exceed the limit provided for in these Rules.

4. Nevertheless, a servant or agent of the carrier shall not be entitled to avail himself of the provisions of this article, if it is proved that the damage resulted from an act or omission of the servant or agent done with intent to cause damage or recklessly and with knowledge that damage would probably result.

ARTICLE V

A carrier shall be at liberty to surrender in whole or in part all or any of his rights and immunities or to increase any of his responsibilities and obligations under these Rules, provided such surrender or increase shall be embodied in the bill of lading issued to the shipper. The provisions of these Rules shall not be applicable to charter parties, but if bills of lading are issued in the case of a ship under a charter party they shall comply with the terms of these Rules. Nothing in these Rules shall be held to prevent the insertion in a bill of lading of any lawful provision regarding general average.

ARTICLE VI

Notwithstanding the provisions of the preceding articles, a carrier, master or agent of the carrier and a shipper shall in regard to any particular goods be at liberty to enter into any agreement in any terms as to the responsibility and liability of the carrier for such goods, and as to the rights and immunities of the carrier in respect of such goods, or his obligation as to seaworthiness, so far as this stipulation is not contrary to public policy, or the care or diligence of his servants or agents in regard to the loading, handling, stowage, carriage, custody, care and discharge of the goods carried by sea, provided that in this case no bill of lading has been or shall be issued and that the terms agreed shall be embodied in a receipt which shall be a non-negotiable document and shall be marked as such.

Any agreement so entered into shall have full legal effect.

Provided that this article shall not apply to ordinary commercial shipments made in the ordinary course of trade, but only to other shipments where the character or condition of the property to be carried or the circumstances, terms and conditions under which the carriage is to be performed are such as reasonably to justify a special agreement.

ARTICLE VII

Nothing herein contained shall prevent a carrier or a shipper from entering into any agreement, stipulation, condition, reservation or exemption as to the responsibility and liability of the carrier or the ship for the loss or damage to, or in connection with, the custody and care and handling of goods prior to the loading on, and subsequent to the discharge from, the ship on which the goods are carried by sea.

ARTICLE VIII

The provisions of these Rules shall not affect the rights and obligations of the carrier under any statute for the time being in force relating to the limitation of the liability of owners of sea-going vessels.

ARTICLE IX

These Rules shall not affect the provisions of any international Convention or national law governing liability for nuclear damage.

ARTICLE X

The provisions of these Rules shall apply to every bill of lading relating to the carriage of goods between ports in two different States if:

- (*a*) the bill of lading is issued in a contracting State, or
- (*b*) the carriage is from a port in a contracting State, or
- (*c*) the contract contained in or evidenced by the bill of lading provides that these Rules or legislation of any State giving effect to them are to govern the contract,

whatever may be the nationality of the ship, the carrier, the shipper, the consignee, or any other interested person.

(The last two paragraphs of this article are not reproduced. They require contracting States to apply the Rules to bills of lading mentioned in the article and authorise them to apply the Rules to other bills of lading.)

Events leading to the Carriage of Goods by Sea Act, 1971, giving effect in the United Kingdom to the Brussels Protocol, 1968.

THIS Act received Royal Assent on the 8th April, 1971, and incorporates the amendments to the Hague Rules 1924 by the Brussels Protocol 1968. The Act supercedes and repeals the Carriage of Goods by Sea Act, 1924, and gives the force of law in the United Kingdom to the Hague Rules as amended by the Brussels Protocol signed at Brussels on the 23rd February, 1968, these Rules being set out in the Schedule to the Act. The Act relates to the carriage of goods by sea in ships where the port of shipment is a port in the United Kingdom, whether or not the carriage is between ports in two different States within the meaning of Article X of the Rules, and is applicable to contracts of carriage expressly or by implication providing for the issue of a bill of lading or any similar document of title. Special note should be made of the words "by implication".

Additionally it should be noted that the 1971 Act provides that the Rules shall be applicable to deck cargo or live animals where the bill of lading or non-negotiable receipt covering such carriage is expressly made subject to the Rules. The Hague Rules as amended by the Brussels Protocol 1968 exclude the application of the Rules to live animals and cargo which by the contract of carriage is stated as being carried on deck and is so carried. To this extent, the international law as amended by the Brussels Protocol 1968 has been varied in the United Kingdom, by the Carriage of Goods by Sea Act, 1971.

Provision is also made for amendment to the limitation of liability provisions of the Brussels Protocol. The Act also provides in particular that there shall not be implied in any contract for the carriage of goods by sea to which the Rules (as amended by the Protocol) apply by virtue of the Act, any absolute undertaking by the carrier to provide a seaworthy ship, so abolishing the absolute warranty of seaworthiness.

Provisions are made for the application of the Act to British possessions etc., namely (a) any colony (not being a colony for whose external relations a country other than the United Kingdom is responsible) and (b) any country outside H.M. Dominions in which Her Majesty has jurisdiction in right of Her Majesty's Government of the United Kingdom. Provision is also made for the extension of the amended Rules of the Brussels Protocol to carriage from ports in British possessions, Isle of Man, Channel Islands etc, the Act also extending to Northern Island.

Particular note must also be taken of the declaration that for the purposes of Article VIII of the Hague Rules as amended by the Brussels Protocol, section 502 of the Merchant Shipping Act 1894 (which as amended by the Merchant Shipping (Liability of Shipowners and Others) Act, 1958, entirely exempts shipowners and others in certain circumstances from liability for loss of, or damage to, goods) is a provision relating to limitation of liability.

So in looking at the international rules relating to bills of lading, reference must also be made to the provisions of the Carriage of Goods by Sea Act, 1971.

THE CARRIAGE OF GOODS BY SEA ACT 1971

An Act to amend the law with respect to the carriage of goods by sea. [*8th April 1971*]

BE it enacted by the Queen's most Excellent Majesty, by and with the advice and consent of the Lords Spiritual and Temporal, and Commons, in this present Parliament assembled, and by the authority of the same, as follows:

1.—(1) In this Act, "the Rules" means the International Convention for the unification of certain rules of law relating to bills of lading signed at Brussels on 25th August 1924, as amended by the Protocol signed at Brussels on 23rd February 1968. Application of Hague Rules as amended.

(2) The provisions of the Rules, as set out in the Schedule to this Act, shall have the force of law.

(3) Without prejudice to subsection (2) above, the said provisions shall have effect (and have the force of law) in relation to and in connection with the carriage of goods by sea in ships where the port of shipment is a port in the United Kingdom, whether or not the carriage is between ports in two different States within the meaning of Article X of the Rules.

(4) Subject to subsection (6) below, nothing in this section shall be taken as applying anything in the Rules to any contract for the carriage of goods by sea, unless the contract expressly or by implication provides for the issue of a bill of lading or any similar document of title.

(5) The Secretary of State may from time to time by order made by statutory instrument specify the respective amounts which for the purposes of paragraph 5 of Article IV of the Rules and of Article IV bis of the Rules are to be taken as equivalent to the sums expressed in francs which are mentioned in sub-paragraph (*a*) of that paragraph.

(6) Without prejudice to Article X(*c*) of the Rules, the Rules shall have the force of law in relation to:

(*a*) any bill of lading if the contract contained in or evidenced by it expressly provides that the Rules shall govern the contract, and

(*b*) any receipt which is a non-negotiable document marked as such if the contract contained in or evidenced by it is a contract for the carriage of goods by sea which expressly provides that the Rules are to govern the contract as if the receipt were a bill of lading.

but subject, where paragraph (*b*) applies, to any necessary modifications and in particular with the omission in Article III of the Rules of the second sentence of paragraph 4 and of paragraph 7.

(7) If and so far as the contract contained in or evidenced by a bill of lading or receipt within paragraph (*a*) or (*b*) of sub-section (6) above applies to deck cargo or live animals, the Rules as given the force of law by that subsection shall have effect as if Article I(*c*) did not exclude deck cargo and live animals.

In this subsection "deck cargo" means cargo which by the contract of carriage is stated as being carried on deck and is so carried.

Contracting States, etc.

2.—(1) If Her Majesty by Order in Council certifies to the following effect, that is to say, that for the purposes of the Rules:

    (*a*)   a State specified in the Order is a contracting State, or is a contracting State in respect of any place or territory so specified;
         or
    (*b*)   any place or territory specified in the Order forms part of a State so specified (whether a contracting State or not).

the Order shall, except so far as it has been superseded by a subsequent Order, be conclusive evidence of the matters so certified.

(2) An Order in Council under this section may be varied or revoked by a subsequent Order in Council.

Absolute warranty of seaworthiness not to be implied in contracts to which Rules apply.

3. There shall not be implied in any contract for the carriage of goods by sea to which the Rules apply by virtue of this Act any absolute undertaking by the carrier of the goods to provide a seaworthy ship.

4.—(1) Her Majesty may by Order in Council direct that this Act shall extend, subject to such exceptions, adaptations and modifications as may be specified in the Order, to all or any of the following territories, that is:

Application of Act to British possessions, etc.

    (*a*)   any colony (not being a colony for whose external relations a country other than the United Kingdom is responsible),
    (*b*)   any country outside Her Majesty's dominions in which Her Majesty has jurisdiction in right of Her Majesty's Government of the United Kingdom.

(2) An Order in Council under this section may contain such transitional and other consequential and incidental provisions as appear to Her Majesty to be expedient, including provisions amending or repealing any legislation about the carriage of goods by sea forming part of the law of any of the territories mentioned in paragraphs (*a*) and (*b*) above.

(3) An Order in Council under this section may be varied or revoked by a subsequent Order in Council.

5.—(1) Her Majesty may by Order in Council provide that section 1(3) of this Act shall have effect as if the reference therein to the United Kingdom included a reference to all or any of the following territories, that is: Extension of application of Rules to carriage from ports in British possessions, etc.

(a) the Isle of Man;

(b) any of the Channel Islands specified in the Order;

(c) any colony specified in the Order (not being a colony for whose external relations a country other than the United Kingdom is responsible);

(d) any associated state (as defined by section 1(3) of the West Indies Act 1967) specified in the Order;

(e) any country specified in the Order, being a country outside Her Majesty's dominions in which Her Majesty has jurisdiction in right of Her Majesty's Government of the United Kingdom.

(2) An Order in Council under this section may be varied or revoked by a subsequent Order in Council.

6.—(1) This Act may be cited as the Carriage of Goods by Sea Act 1971. Supplemental.

(2) It is hereby declared that this Act extends to Northern Ireland.

(3) The following enactments shall be repealed, that is:

(a) the Carriage of Goods by Sea Act 1924,

(b) section 12(4)(a) of the Nuclear Installations Act 1965, and without prejudice to section 38(1) of the Interpretation Act 1889, the reference to the said Act of 1924 in section 1(1)(i)(ii) of the Hovercraft Act 1968 shall include a reference to this Act.

(4) It is hereby declared that for the purposes of Article VIII of the Rules section 502 of the Merchant Shipping Act 1894 (which, as amended by the Merchant Shipping (Liability of Shipowners and Others) Act 1958, entirely exempts shipowners and others in certain circumstances from liability for loss of, or damage to, goods) is a provision relating to limitation of liability.

(5) This Act shall come into force on such day as Her Majesty may by Order in Council appoint, and, for the purposes of the transition from the law in force immediately before the day appointed under this subsection to the provisions of this Act, the Order appointing the day may provide that those provisions shall have effect subject to such transitional provisions as may be contained in the Order.

Events leading to the Hamburg Rules agreed at the United Nations Conference on the Carriage of Goods by Sea, 6 — 31 March, 1978

ALMOST before the ink was dry at the signing of the Brussels Protocol in 1968, positive steps were being taken by the United Nations Conference on Trade and Development to amend the Hague Rules in their entirety. The Committee on Shipping established a Working Group on International Shipping Legislation. First priority was given to a study of bills of lading. This study took the form of a review of the economic and commercial aspects of international legislation and practices in the field of bills of lading from the standpoint of their conformity with the needs of economic development, in particular of the developing countries, and it made appropriate recommendations as regards, *inter alia*, the following subjects:

(a) Principles and rules governing bills of lading
    (i) Applicable law and forum including arbitration
    (ii) Conflict of laws between conventions and national legislation
    (iii) Responsibilities and liabilities in respect of carriage of goods
    (iv) Voyage deviation and delays.
(b) Study of standard forms of documentation, including an analysis of standard forms of documentation, including an analysis of common terms
(c) Trade customs and usages relating to bills of lading
(d) Third party interests at ports of call.

This list of topics called for the examination of four distinct elements (1) general problems arising from the functioning of international legislation and practices concerning bills of lading, (2) the more specifically economic and commercial aspects of the above problems (3) the extent to which the international legislation and practices conformed with the balancing of equities between the owners and carriers of cargo, again with particular concern for the position of the developing countries (4) the specific provisions of the Hague Rules and associated national laws which the UNCTAD Shipping Committee found had given rise to difficulties.

In response to the wishes of the Working Group, the UNCTAD secretariat prepared a report, in which the secretariat commented that bearing in mind the misgivings of many countries as to the trends which they discerned in the existing maritime laws (e.g. possible bias in favour of any of the parties to the contract of ocean carriage), the secretariat attempted in the report to clarify the needs and aspirations of shipowners and cargo owners as to their expectations from the contract of ocean carriage, attention being drawn to the special needs of developing countries.

Two principal issues required examination (1) when goods are lost or damaged in the course of ocean carriage, is it always known in which cases the carrier has to pay and in which the loss remains where it falls, namely on the shipper or his successor, the holder of the bill of lading, or the insurer? (2) What conditions of sea carriage are most consonant with public policy and economic needs? This latter issue could be broken down into several sub-questions, namely (1) should the carrier or the cargo owner bear all of the risk, or should the risk be apportioned between them? (2) If so, how? (3) How fair is the present apportionment of the risk of loss or damage to goods carried by sea? (4) Is the legal protection given to affected interests in contracts of carriage consonant with what these interests may expect today? (5) Are the existing laws so framed that they tend to prejudice the interests of the developing countries? (6) To what extent can the existing balance of liabilities and immunities under the Hague Rules be changed without causing detrimental economic distortions?

The evidence of the need to revise the Hague Rules, beyond that achieved by the Brussels Protocol, 1968, came from several sources. Firstly there were the complaints made in response to the enquiries of the UNCTAD secretariat. Secondly, from a study of standard texts and periodicals. And thirdly there was the result of the analysis of commercial and economic aspects and consequences, and of the analysis of the Hague Rules themselves.

The main grounds for concern were: (a) Uncertainty in the application of laws, in relation to difficulties in establishing where and how the loss or damage to goods occurred — burden of proof — allocation of responsibility for loss or damage to cargo, all of which was the subject of complaint by both shipowning and cargo interests. (b) The continued retention in bills of lading of exoneration clauses of doubtful validity, and the existence of restrictive exemption and time-limitation clauses in the terms under which cargo is deposited with warehouse and port authorities. (c) Exemptions in the Hague Rules which are peculiar to ocean carriage, in cases where the liability should logically be borne by the ocean carrier, such as those which exempt him from liability in respect of the negligence of his servants and agents in the navigation and management of the vessel, and in respect of perils of the sea etc. (d) The uncertainties caused by the interpretation of terms used in the Hague Rules, such as "reasonable deviation", "due diligence", "properly and carefully", "in any event", "subject to". (e) The ambiguities surrounding the seaworthiness of vessels for the carriage of goods. (f) The unit limitation of liability. (g) Jurisdiction and arbitration clauses. (h) The insufficient legal protection for cargoes with special characteristics that require special stowage, adequate ventilation, etc., and cargoes requiring deck shipment. (i) Clauses which permit carriers to divert vessels, and to tranship or land the goods short of or beyond the port of destination specified in the bill of lading at the risk and expense of the cargo owners. (j) Clauses which entitle carriers to deliver goods into the custody of shore custodians on terms which make it almost impossible to obtain settlements of cargo claims from either the carrier or the warehouse.

The opinion was formed that the Hague Rules provided an excessive number of opportunities for the shipowner to legally avoid liability for loss of cargo and so to reject the claim made by the cargo owner. It was found also that this situation existed because of the unit limitation, whereby the liability of the shipowner, even where full responsibility was admitted, was limited to a fixed amount irrespective of the value of the goods lost or damaged. It has to be mentioned here that there is an exception to this limitation of liability if the cargo owner declares the value of the goods before shipment and the value is entered in the bill of lading, but cargo owners would only take this measure in very special circumstances, because of the increased freight charges that would follow such a declaration.

It was felt that there were strong grounds for revising the Hague Rules or for the establishment of a new international convention. The secretariat made a long and detailed report based upon the findings of the Working Group on International Shipping Legislation, in which the Hague Rules were examined at great length, rule by rule, detailed proposals being made as to the manner in which the Hague Rules should be amended, and the reasons for the conclusions reached. Thereafter, a Working Group established by the United Nations Commission on International Trade Law, (UNCITRAL) produced a draft Convention on the Carriage of Goods by Sea.

The Draft Convention on the Carriage of Goods by Sea, together with comments submitted by governments and international organisations, were considered by UNCITRAL at its ninth session, held in New York from April 12 to May 7, 1976. The final text was then considered by the General Assembly of the United Nations when it was decided that an international conference should be convened in 1978, in New York, or at any other suitable place, to consider the question of the carriage of goods by sea and to embody the results of the work of UNCITRAL in an international convention. Subsequently the Secretary General of the United Nations received, and accepted, an invitation from the Government of the Federal Republic of Germany to hold the conference at Hamburg. The Conference was held in March 1978, when the new rules, amending the Hague Rules, were adopted. These were the Hamburg Rules, which will come into force on the first day of the month following the expiration of one year from the date of the deposit of the 20th instrument of ratification, acceptance, approval or accession.

HAMBURG RULES 1978
ANNEX I
UNITED NATIONS CONVENTION ON THE CARRIAGE OF GOODS BY SEA, 1978

Signed at Hamburg on the 31st March 1978

Preamble

THE STATES PARTIES TO THIS CONVENTION,

HAVING RECOGNIZED the desirability of determining by agreement certain rules relating to the carriage of goods by sea.

HAVE DECIDED to conclude a Convention for this purpose and have thereto agreed as follows:

PART I. GENERAL PROVISIONS
Article 1. Definitions

In this Convention:

1. "Carrier" means any person by whom or in whose name a contract of carriage of goods by sea has been concluded with a shipper.

2. "Actual carrier" means any person to whom the performance of the carriage of the goods, or of part of the carriage, has been entrusted by the carrier, and includes any other person to whom such performance has been entrusted.

3. "Shipper" means any person by whom or in whose name or on whose behalf a contract of carriage of goods by sea has been concluded with a carrier, or any person by whom or in whose name or on whose behalf the goods are actually delivered to the carrier in relation to the contract of carriage by sea.

4. "Consignee" means the person entitled to take delivery of the goods.

5. "Goods" includes live animals; where the goods are consolidated in a container, pallet or similar article of transport or where they are packed, "goods" includes such article of transport or packaging if supplied by the shipper.

6. "Contract of carriage by sea" means any contract whereby the carrier undertakes against payment of freight to carry goods by sea from one port to another; however, a contract which involves carriage by sea and also carriage by some other means is

deemed to be a contract of carriage by sea for the purposes of this Convention only in so far as it relates to the carriage by sea.

7. "Bill of lading" means a document which evidences a contract of carriage by sea and the taking over or loading of the goods by the carrier, and by which the carrier undertakes to deliver the goods against surrender of the document. A provision in the document that the goods are to be delivered to the order of a named person, or to order, or to bearer, constitutes such an undertaking.

8. "Writing" includes, *inter alia*, telegram and telex.

Article 2. Scope of application

1. The provisions of this Convention are applicable to all contracts of carriage by sea between two different States, if:
   (a) the port of loading as provided for in the contract of carriage by sea is located in a Contracting State, or
   (b) the port of discharge as provided for in the contract of carriage by sea is located in a Contracting State, or
   (c) one of the optional ports of discharge provided for in the contract of carriage by sea is the actual port of discharge and such port is located in a Contracting State, or
   (d) the bill of lading or other document evidencing the contract of carriage by sea is issued in a Contracting State, or
   (e) the bill of lading or other document evidencing the contract of carriage by sea provides that the provisions of this Convention or the legislation of any State giving effect to them are to govern the contract.

2. The provisions of this Convention are applicable without regard to the nationality of the ship, the carrier, the actual carrier, the shipper, the consignee or any other interested person.

3. The provisions of this Convention are not applicable to charter-parties. However, where a bill of lading is issued pursuant to a charter-party, the provisions of the Convention apply to such a bill of lading if it governs the relation between the carrier and the holder of the bill of lading, not being the charterer.

4. If a contract provides for future carriage of goods in a series of shipments during an agreed period, the provisions of this Convention apply to each shipment. However, where a shipment is made under a charter-party, the provisions of paragraph 3 of this article apply.

Article 3. Interpretation of the Convention

In the interpretation and application of the provisions of this Convention regard shall be had to its international character and to the need to promote uniformity.

PART II. LIABILITY OF THE CARRIER

Article 4. Period of responsibility

1. The responsibility of the carrier for the goods under this Convention covers the period during which the carrier is in charge of the goods at the port of loading, during the carriage and at the port of discharge.

2. For the purpose of paragraph 1 of this article, the carrier is deemed to be in charge of the goods
   (a) from the time he has taken over the goods from:
      (i)   the shipper, or a person acting on his behalf; or
      (ii) an authority or other third party to whom, pursuant to law or regulations applicable at the port of loading, the goods must be handed over for shipment;
   (b) until the time he has delivered the goods:
      (i)   by handing over the goods to the consignee; or
      (ii) in cases where the consignee does not receive the goods from the carrier, by placing them at the disposal of the consignee in accordance with the contract or with the law or with the usage of the particular trade, applicable at the port of discharge; or
      (iii) by handing over the goods to an authority or other third party to whom, pursuant to law or regulations applicable at the port of discharge, the goods must be handed over.

3. In paragraphs 1 and 2 of this article, reference to the carrier or to the consignee means, in addition to the carrier or the consignee, the servants or agents, respectively of the carrier or the consignee.

Article 5. Basis of liability

1. The carrier is liable for loss resulting from loss of or damage to the goods, as well as from delay in delivery, if the occurrence which caused the loss, damage or delay took place while the goods were in his charge as defined in article 4, unless the carrier proves that he, his servants or agents took all measures that could reasonably be required to avoid the occurrence and its consequences.

2. Delay in delivery occurs when the goods have not been delivered at the port of discharge provided for in the contract of carriage by sea within the time expressly agreed upon or, in the absence of such agreement, within the time which it would be reasonable to require of a diligent carrier, having regard to the circumstances of the case.

3. The person entitled to make a claim for the loss of goods

may treat the goods as lost if they have not been delivered as required by article 4 within 60 consecutive days following the expiry of the time for delivery according to paragraph 2 of this article.

4. (a) The carrier is liable
   (i) for loss of or damage to the goods or delay in delivery caused by fire, if the claimant proves that the fire arose from fault or neglect on the part of the carrier, his servants or agents;
   (ii) for such loss, damage or delay in delivery which is proved by the claimant to have resulted from the fault or neglect of the carrier, his servants or agents, in taking all measures that could reasonably be required to put out the fire and avoid or mitigate its consequences.

   (b) In case of fire on board the ship affecting the goods, if the claimant or the carrier so desires, a survey in accordance with shipping practices must be held into the cause and circumstances of the fire, and a copy of the surveyor's report shall be made available on demand to the carrier and the claimant.

5. With respect to live animals, the carrier is not liable for loss, damage or delay in delivery resulting from any special risks inherent in that kind of carriage. If the carrier proves that he has complied with any special instructions given to him by the shipper respecting the animals and that, in the circumstances of the case, the loss, damage or delay in delivery could be attributed to such risks, it is presumed that the loss, damage or delay in delivery was so caused, unless there is proof that all or a part of the loss, damage or delay in delivery resulted from fault or neglect on the part of the carrier, his servants or agents.

6. The carrier is not liable, except in general average, where loss, damage or delay in delivery resulted from measures to save life or from reasonable measures to save property at sea.

7. Where fault or neglect on the part of the carrier, his servants or agents combines with another cause to produce loss, damage or delay in delivery the carrier is liable only to the extent that the loss, damage or delay in delivery is attributable to such fault or neglect, provided that the carrier proves the amount of the loss, damage or delay in delivery not attributable thereto.

Article 6. Limits of liability

1. (a) The liability of the carrier for loss resulting from loss of or damage to goods according to the provisions of article 5 is limited to an amount equivalent to 835 units of account per package or other shipping unit or 2.5 units of

account per kilogramme of gross weight of the goods lost or damaged, whichever is the higher.

(b) The liability of the carrier for delay in delivery according to the provisions of article 5 is limited to an amount equivalent to two and a half times the freight payable for the goods delayed, but not exceeding the total freight payable under the contract of carriage of goods by sea.

(c) In no case shall the aggregate liability of the carrier, under both subparagraphs (a) and (b) of this paragraph, exceed the limitation which would be established under subparagraph (a) of this paragraph for total loss of the goods with respect to which such liability was incurred.

2. For the purpose of calculating which amount is the higher in accordance with paragraph 1 (a) of this article, the following rules apply:

(a) Where a container, pallet or similar article of transport is used to consolidate goods, the package or other shipping units enumerated in the bill of lading, if issued, or otherwise in any other document evidencing the contract of carriage by sea, as packed in such article of transport are deemed packages or shipping units. Except as aforesaid the goods in such article of transport are deemed one shipping unit.

(b) In cases where the article of transport itself has been lost or damaged, that article of transport, if not owned or otherwise supplied by the carrier, is considered one separate shipping unit.

3. Unit of account means the unit of account mentioned in article 26.

4. By agreement between the carrier and the shipper, limits of liability exceeding those provided for in paragraph 1 may be fixed.

Article 7. Application to non-contractual claims

1. The defences and limits of liability provided for in this Convention apply in any action against the carrier in respect of loss or damage to the goods covered by the contract of carriage by sea, as well as of delay in delivery whether the action is founded in contract, in tort or otherwise.

2. If such an action is brought against a servant or agent of the carrier, such servant or agent, if he proves that he acted within the scope of his employment, is entitled to avail himself of the defences and limits of liability which the carrier is entitled to invoke under this Convention.

3. Except as provided in article 8, the aggregate of the amounts recoverable from the carrier and from any persons referred to in

paragraph 2 of this article shall not exceed the limits of liability provided for in this Convention.

Article 8. Loss of right to limit responsibility

1. The carrier is not entitled to the benefit of the limitation of liability provided for in article 6 if it is proved that the loss, damage or delay in delivery resulted from an act or omission of the carrier done with the intent to cause such loss, damage or delay, or recklessly and with knowledge that such loss, damage or delay would probably result.

2. Notwithstanding the provisions of paragraph 2 of article 7, a servant or agent of the carrier is not entitled to the benefit of the limitation of liability provided for in article 6 if it is proved that the loss, damage or delay in delivery resulted from an act or omission of such servant or agent, done with the intent to cause such loss, damage or delay, or recklessly and with knowledge that such loss, damage or delay would probably result.

Article 9. Deck cargo

1. The carrier is entitled to carry the goods on deck only if such carriage is in accordance with an agreement with the shipper or with the usage of the particular trade or is required by statutory rules or regulations.

2. If the carrier and the shipper have agreed that the goods shall or may be carried on deck, the carrier must insert in the bill of lading or other document evidencing the contract of carriage by sea a statement to that effect. In the absence of such a statement the carrier has the burden of proving that an agreement for carriage on deck has been entered into; however, the carrier is not entitled to invoke such an agreement against a third party, including a consignee, who has acquired the bill of lading in good faith.

3. Where the goods have been carried on deck contrary to the provisions of paragraph 1 of this article or where the carrier may not under paragraph 2 of this article invoke an agreement for carriage on deck, the carrier, notwithstanding the provisions of paragraph 1 of article 5, is liable for loss of or damage to the goods, as well as for delay in delivery, resulting solely from the carriage on deck, and the extent of his liability is to be determined in accordance with the provisions of article 6 or article 8 of this Convention, as the case may be.

4. Carriage of goods on deck contrary to express agreement for carriage under deck is deemed to be an act or omission of the carrier within the meaning of article 8.

Article 10. Liability of the carrier and actual carrier

1. Where the performance of the carriage of part thereof has been entrusted to an actual carrier, whether or not in pursuance of a liberty under the contract of carriage by sea to do so, the carrier nevertheless remains responsible for the entire carriage according to the provisions of this Convention. The carrier is responsible, in relation to the carriage performed by the actual carrier, for the acts and omissions of the actual carrier and of his servants and agents acting within the scope of their employment.

2. All the provisions of this Convention governing the responsibility of the carrier also apply to the responsibility of the actual carrier for the carriage performed by him. The provisions of paragraphs 2 and 3 of article 7 and of paragraph 2 of article 8 apply if an action is brought against a servant or agent of the actual carrier.

3. Any special agreement under which the carrier assumes obligations not imposed by this Convention or waives rights conferred by this Convention affects the actual carrier only if agreed to by him expressly and in writing. Whether or not the actual carrier has so agreed, the carrier nevertheless remains bound by the obligations or waivers resulting from such special agreement.

4. Where and to the extent that both the carrier and the actual carrier are liable, their liability is joint and several.

5. The aggregate of the amounts recoverable from the carrier, the actual carrier and their servants and agents shall not exceed the limits of liability provided for in this Convention.

6. Nothing in this article shall prejudice any right of recourse as between the carrier and the actual carrier.

Article 11. Through carriage

1. Notwithstanding the provisions of paragraph 1 of article 10, where a contract of carriage by sea provides explicitly that a specified part of the carriage covered by the said contract is to be performed by a named person other than the carrier, the contract may also provide that the carrier is not liable for loss, damage or delay in delivery caused by an occurrence which takes place while the goods are in the charge of the actual carrier during such part of the carriage. Nevertheless, any stipulation limiting or excluding such liability is without effect if no judicial proceedings can be instituted against the actual carrier in a court competent under paragraph 1 or 2 of article 21. The burden of proving that any loss, damage or delay in delivery has been caused by such an occurrence rests upon the carrier.

2. The actual carrier is responsible in accordance with the

provisions of paragraph 2 of article 10 for loss, damage or delay in delivery caused by an occurrence which takes place while the goods are in his charge.

PART III. LIABILITY OF THE SHIPPER

Article 12. General rule

The shipper is not lible for loss sustained by the carrier or the actual carrier, or for damage sustained by the ship, unless such loss or damage was caused by the fault or neglect of the shipper, his servants or agents. Nor is any servant or agent of the shipper liable for such loss or damage unless the loss or damage was caused by fault or neglect on his part.

Article 13. Special rules on dangerous goods

1. The shipper must mark or label in a suitable manner dangerous goods as dangerous.
2. Where the shipper hands over dangerous goods to the carrier or an actual carrier, as the case may be, the shipper must inform him of the dangerous character of the goods and, if necessary, of the precautions to be taken. If the shipper fails to do so and such carrier or actual carrier does not otherwise have knowledge of their dangerous character:
   - (a) the shipper is liable to the carrier and any actual carrier for the loss resulting from the shipment of such goods, and
   - (b) the goods may at any time be unloaded, destroyed or rendered innocuous, as the circumstances may require, without payment of compensation.
3. The provisions of paragraph 2 of this article may not be invoked by any person if during the carriage he has taken the goods in his charge with knowledge of their dangerous character.
4. If, in cases where the provisions of paragraph 2, subparagraph (b), of this article do not apply or may not be invoked, dangerous goods become an actual danger to life or property, they may be unloaded, destroyed or rendered innocuous, as the circumstances may require, without payment of compensation except where there is an obligation to contribute in general average or where the carrier is liable in accordance with the provisions of article 5.

PART IV. TRANSPORT DOCUMENTS

Article 14. Issue of bill of lading

1. When the carrier or the actual carrier takes the goods in his charge, the carrier must, on demand of the shipper, issue to the shipper a bill of lading.

2. The bill of lading may be signed by a person having authority from the carrier. A bill of lading signed by the master of the ship carrying the goods is deemed to have been signed on behalf of the carrier.

3. The signature on the bill of lading may be in handwriting, printed in facsimile, perforated, stamped, in symbols, or made by any other mechanical or electronic means, if not inconsistent with the law of the country where the bill of lading is issued.

Article 15. Contents of bill of lading

1. The bill of lading must include, *inter alia*, the following particulars:

   (a) the general nature of the goods, the leading marks necessary for identification of the goods, an express statement, if applicable, as to the dangerous character of the goods, the number of packages or pieces, and the weight of the goods or their quantity otherwise expressed, all such particulars as furnished by the shipper;

   (b) the apparent condition of the goods;

   (c) the name and principal place of business of the carrier;

   (d) the name of the shipper;

   (e) the consignee if named by the shipper;

   (f) the port of loading under the contract of carriage by sea and the date on which the goods were taken over by the carrier at the port of loading;

   (g) the port of discharge under the contract of carriage by sea;

   (h) the number of originals of the bill of lading, if more than one;

   (i) the place of issuance of the bill of lading;

   (j) the signature of the carrier or a person acting on his behalf;

   (k) the freight to the extent payable by the consignee or other indication that freight is payable by him;

   (l) the statement referred to in paragraph 3 of article 23;

   (m) the statement, if applicable, that the goods shall or may be carried on deck;

   (n) the date or the period of delivery of the goods at the port of discharge if expressly agreed upon between the parties; and

   (o) any increased limit or limits of liability where agreed in accordance with paragraph 4 of article 6.

2. After the goods have been loaded on board, if the shipper so demands, the carrier must issue to the shipper a "shipped" bill of lading which, in addition to the particulars required under paragraph 1 of this article, must state that the goods are on board

a named ship or ships, and the date or dates of loading. If the carrier has previously issued to the shipper a bill of lading or other document of title with respect to any of such goods, on request of the carrier, the shipper must surrender such document in exchange for a "shipped" bill of lading. The carrier may amend any previously issued document in order to meet the shipper's demand for a "shipped" bill of lading if, as amended, such document includes all the information required to be contained in a "shipped" bill of lading.

3. The absence in the bill of lading of one or more particulars referred to in this article does not affect the legal character of the document as a bill of lading provided that it nevertheless meets the requirements set out in paragraph 7 of article 1.

Article 16. Bills of Lading: reservations and evidentiary effect

1. If the bill of lading contains particulars concerning the general nature, leading marks, number of packages or pieces, weight or quantity of the goods which the carrier or other person issuing the bill of lading on his behalf knows or has reasonable grounds to suspect do not accurately represent the goods actually taken over or, where a "shipped" bill of lading is issued, loaded, or if he had no reasonable means of checking such particulars, the carrier or such other person must insert in the bill of lading a reservation specifying these inaccuracies, grounds of suspicion or the absence of reasonable means of checking.

2. If the carrier or other person issuing the bill of lading on his behalf fails to note on the bill of lading the apparent condition of the goods, he is deemed to have noted on the bill of lading that the goods were in apparent good condition.

3. Except for particulars in respect of which and to the extent to which a reservation permitted under paragraph 1 of this article has been entered:

   (a) the bill of lading is *prima facie* evidence of the taking over or, where a "shipped" bill of lading is issued, loading, by the carrier of the goods as described in the bill of lading; and

   (b) proof to the contrary by the carrier is not admissible if the bill of lading has been transferred to a third party, including a consignee, who in good faith has acted in reliance on the description of the goods therein.

4. A bill of lading which does not, as provided in paragraph 1, subparagraph (k) of article 15, set forth the freight or otherwise indicate that freight is payable by the consignee or does not set forth demurrage incurred at the port of loading payable by the consignee, is *prima facie* evidence that no freight or such demurrage is payable by him. However, proof to the contrary by the carrier is not admissible when the bill of lading has been transferred to a third party, including a consignee, who in good faith has acted in reliance on the absence in the bill of lading of any such indication.

Article 17. Guarantees by the shipper

1. The shipper is deemed to have guaranteed to the carrier the accuracy of particulars relating to the general nature of the goods, their marks, number, weight and quantity as furnished by him for insertion in the bill of lading. The shipper must indemnify the carrier against the loss resulting from inaccuracies in such particulars. The shipper remains liable even if the bill of lading has been transferred by him. The right of the carrier to such indemnity in no way limits his liability under the contract of

carriage by sea to any person other than the shipper.

2. Any letter of guarantee or agreement by which the shipper undertakes to indemnify the carrier against loss resulting from the issuance of the bill of lading by the carrier, or by a person acting on his behalf, without entering a reservation relating to particulars furnished by the shipper for insertion in the bill of lading, or to the apparent condition of the goods, is void and of no effect as against any third party, including a consignee, to whom the bill of lading has been transferred.

3. Such letter of guarantee or agreement is valid as against the shipper unless the carrier or the person acting on his behalf, by omitting the reservation referred to in paragraph 2 of this article, intends to defraud a third party, including a consignee, who acts in reliance on the description of the goods in the bill of lading. In the latter case, if the reservation omitted relates to particulars furnished by the shipper for insertion in the bill of lading, the carrier has no right of indemnity from the shipper pursuant to paragraph 1 of this article.

4. In the case of intended fraud referred to in paragraph 3 of this article the carrier is liable, without the benefit of the limitation of liability provided for in this Convention, for the loss incurred by a third party, including a consignee, because he has acted in reliance on the description of the goods in the bill of lading.

Article 18. Documents other than bills of lading

Where a carrier issues a document other than a bill of lading to evidence the receipt of the goods to be carried, such a document is *prima facie* evidence of the conclusion of the contract of carriage by sea and the taking over by the carrier of the goods as therein described.

PART V. CLAIMS AND ACTIONS

Article 19. Notice of loss, damage or delay

1. Unless notice of loss or damage, specifying the general nature of such loss or damage, is given in writing by the consignee to the carrier not later than the working day after the day when the goods were handed over to the consignee, such handing over is *prima facie* evidence of the delivery by the carrier of the goods as described in the document of transport or if no such document has been issued, in good condition.

2. Where the loss or damage is not apparent, the provisions of paragraph 1 of this article apply correspondingly if notice in writing is not given within 15 consecutive days after the day when the goods were handed over to the consignee.

3. If the state of the goods at the time they were handed over to the consignee has been the subject of a joint survey or inspection by the parties, notice in writing need not be given of loss or damage ascertained during such survey or inspection.

4. In the case of any actual or apprehended loss or damage the carrier and the consignee must give all reasonable facilities to each other for inspecting and tallying the goods.

5. No compensation shall be payable for loss resulting from delay in delivery unless a notice has been given in writing to the carrier within 60 consecutive days after the day when the goods were handed over to the consignee.

6. If the goods have been delivered by an actual carrier, any notice given under this article to him shall have the same effect as if it had been given to the carrier, and any notice given to the carrier shall have effect as if given to such actual carrier.

7. Unless notice of loss or damage, specifying the general nature of the loss or damage, is given in writing by the carrier or actual carrier to the shipper not later than 90 consecutive days after the occurrence of such loss or damage or after the delivery of the goods in accordance with paragraph 2 of article 4, whichever is later, the failure to give such notice is *prima facie* evidence that the carrier or the actual carrier has sustained no loss or damage due to the fault or neglect of the shipper, his servants or agents.

8. For the purpose of this article, notice given to a person acting on the carrier's or the actual carrier's behalf, including the master or the officer in charge of the ship, or to a person acting on the shipper's behalf is deemed to have been given to the carrier, to the actual carrier or to the shipper, respectively.

Article 20. Limitation of actions

1. Any action relating to carriage of goods under this Convention is time-barred if judicial or arbitral proceedings have not been instituted within a period of two years.

2. The limitation period commences on the day on which the carrier has delivered the goods or part thereof or, in cases where no goods have been delivered, on the last day on which the goods should have been delivered.

3. The day on which the limitation period commences is not included in the period.

4. The person against whom a claim is made may at any time during the running of the limitation period extend that period by a declaration in writing to the claimant. This period may be further extended by another declaration or declarations.

5. An action for indemnity by a person held liable may be instituted even after the expiration of the limitation period provided for in the preceding paragraphs if instituted within the time allowed by the law of the State where proceedings are

instituted. However, the time allowed shall not be less than 90 days commencing from the day when the person instituting such action for indemnity has settled the claim or has been served with process in the action against himself.

Article 21. Jurisdiction

1. In judicial proceedings relating to carriage of goods under this Convention the plaintiff, at his option, may institute an action in a court which, according to the law of the State where the court is situated, is competent and within the jurisdiction of which is situated one of the following places:
    (a) the principal place of business or, in the absence thereof, the habitual residence of the defendant; or
    (b) the place where the contract was made provided that the defendant has there a place of business, branch or agency through which the contract was made; or
    (c) the port of loading or the port of discharge; or
    (d) any additional place designated for that purpose in the contract of carriage by sea.

2. (a) Notwithstanding the preceding provisions of this article, an action may be instituted in the courts of any port or place in a Contracting State at which the carrying vessel or any other vessel of the same ownership may have been arrested in accordance with applicable rules of the law of that State and of international law. However, in such a case, at the petition of the defendant, the claimant must remove the action, at his choice, to one of the jurisdictions referred to in paragraph 1 of this article for the determination of the claim, but before such removal the defendant must furnish security sufficient to ensure payment of any judgement that may subsequently be awarded to the claimant in the action.

    (b) All questions relating to the sufficiency or otherwise of the security shall be determined by the court of the port or place of the arrest.

3. No judicial proceedings relating to carriage of goods under this Convention may be instituted in a place not specified in paragraph 1 or 2 of this article. The provisions of this paragraph do not constitute an obstacle to the jurisdiction of the Contracting States for provisional or protective measures.

4. (a) Where an action has been instituted in a court competent under paragraph 1 or 2 of this article or where judgement has been delivered by such a court, no new action may be started between the same parties on the same grounds unless the judgement of the court before which the first action was instituted is not en-

forceable in the country in which the new proceedings are instituted;

(b) for the purpose of this article the institution of measures with a view to obtaining enforcement of a judgement is not to be considered as the starting of a new action;

(c) for the purpose of this article, the removal of an action to a different court within the same country, or to a court in another country, in accordance with paragraph 2 (a) of this article, is not to be considered as the starting of a new action.

5. Notwithstanding the provisions of the preceding paragraphs, an agreement made by the parties, after a claim under the contract of carriage by sea has arisen, which designates the place where the claimant may institute an action, is effective.

Article 22. Arbitration

1. Subject to the provisions of this article, parties may provide by agreement evidenced in writing that any dispute that may arise relating to carriage of goods under this Convention shall be referred to arbitration.

2. Where a charter-party contains a provision that disputes arising thereunder shall be referred to arbitration and a bill of lading issued pursuant to the charter-party does not contain a special annotation providing that such provision shall be binding upon the holder of the bill of lading, the carrier may not invoke such provision as against a holder having acquired the bill of lading in good faith.

3. The arbitration proceedings shall, at the option of the claimant, be instituted as one of the following places:

(a) a place in a State within whose territory is situated:

(i) the principal place of business of the defendant or, in the absence thereof, the habitual residence of the defendant; or

(ii) the place where the contract was made, provided that the defendant has there a place of business, branch or agency through which the contract was made; or

(iii) the port of loading or the port of discharge; or

(b) any place designated for that purpose in the arbitration clause or agreement.

4. The arbitrator or arbitration tribunal shall apply the rules of this Convention.

5. The provisions of paragraphs 3 and 4 of this article are deemed to be part of every arbitration clause or agreement, and any term of such clause or agreement which is inconsistent therewith is null and void.

6. Nothing in this article affects the validity of an agreement

relating to arbitration made by the parties after the claim under the contract of carriage by sea has arisen.

PART VI. SUPPLEMENTARY PROVISIONS

Article 23. Contractual stipulations

1. Any stipulation in a contract of carriage by sea, in a bill of lading, or in any other document evidencing the contract of carriage by sea is null and void to the extent that it derogates, directly or indirectly, from the provisions of this Convention. The nullity of such a stipulation does not affect the validity of the other provisions of the contract or document of which it forms a part. A clause assigning benefit of insurance of the goods in favour of the carrier, or any similar clause, is null and void.

2. Notwithstanding the provisions of paragraph 1 of this article, a carrier may increase his responsibilities and obligations under this Convention.

3. Where a bill of lading or any other document evidencing the contract of carriage by sea is issued, it must contain a statement that the carriage is subject to the provisions of this Convention which nullify any stipulation derogating therefrom to the detriment of the shipper or the consignee.

4. Where the claimant in respect of the goods has incurred loss as a result of a stipulation which is null and void by virtue of the present article, or as a result of the omission of the statement referred to in paragraph 3 of this article, the carrier must pay compensation to the extent required in order to give the claimant compensation in accordance with the provisions of this Convention for any loss of or damage to the goods as well as for delay in delivery. The carrier must, in addition, pay compensation for costs incurred by the claimant for the purpose of exercising his right, provided that costs incurred in the action where the foregoing provision is invoked are to be determined in accordance with the law of the State where proceedings are instituted.

Article 24. General average

1. Nothing in this Convention shall prevent the application of provisions in the contract of carriage by sea or national law regarding the adjustment of general average.

2. With the exception of article 20, the provisions of this Convention relating to the liability of the carrier for loss of or damage to the goods also determine whether the consignee may refuse contribution in general average and the liability of the carrier to indemnify the consignee in respect of any such contribution made or any salvage paid.

Article 25. Other conventions

1. This Convention does not modify the rights or duties of the carrier, the actual carrier and their servants and agents, provided for in international conventions or national law relating to the limitation of liability of owners of seagoing ships.

2. The provisions of articles 21 and 22 of this Convention do not prevent the application of the mandatory provisions of any other multilateral convention already in force at the date of this Convention relating to matters dealt with in the said articles, provided that the dispute arises exclusively between parties having their principal place of business in States members of such other convention. However, this paragraph does not affect the application of paragraph 4 of article 22 of this Convention.

3. No liability shall arise under the provisions of this Convention for damage caused by a nuclear incident if the operator of a nuclear installation is liable for such damage:

   (a) under either the Paris Convention of 29 July 1960 on Third Party Liability in the Field of Nuclear Energy as amended by the Additional Protocol of 28 January 1964 or the Vienna Convention of 21 May 1963 on Civil Liability for Nuclear Damage, or

   (b) by virtue of national law governing the liability for such damage, provided that such law is in all respects as favourable to persons who may suffer damage as either the Paris or Vienna Conventions.

4. No liability shall arise under the provisions of this Convention for any loss of or damage to or delay in delivery of luggage for which the carrier is responsible under any international convention or national law relating to the carriage of passengers and their luggage by sea.

5. Nothing contained in this Convention prevents a Contracting State from applying any other international convention which is already in force at the date of this Convention and which applies mandatorily to contracts of carriage of goods primarily by a mode of transport other than transport by sea. This provision also applies to any subsequent revision or amendment of such international convention.

Article 26. Unit of account

1. The unit of account referred to in article 6 of this Convention is the Special Drawing Right as defined by the International Monetary Fund. The amounts mentioned in article 6 are to be converted into the national currency of a State according to the value of such currency at the date of judgement or the date agreed upon by the parties. The value of a national

currency, in terms of the Special Drawing Right, of a Contracting State which is a member of the International Monetary Fund is to be calculated in accordance with the method of valuation applied by the International Monetary Fund in effect at the date in question for its operations and transactions. The value of a national currency in terms of the Special Drawing Right of a Contracting State which is not a member of the International Monetary Fund is to be calculated in a manner determined by that State.

2. Nevertheless, those States which are not members of the International Monetary Fund and whose law does not permit the application of the provisions of paragraph 1 of this article may, at the time of signature, or at the time of ratification, acceptance, approval or accession or at any time thereafter, declare that the limits of liability provided for in this Convention to be applied in their territories shall be fixed as:

12,500 monetary units per package or other shipping unit or 37.5 monetary units per kilogramme of gross weight of the goods.

3. The monetary unit referred to in paragraph 2 of this article corresponds to sixty-five and a half milligrammes of gold of millesinal fineness nine hundred. The conversion of the amounts referred to in paragraph 2 into the national currency is to be made according to the law of the State concerned.

4. The calculation mentioned in the last sentence of paragraph 1 and the conversion mentioned in paragraph 3 of this article is to be made in such a manner as to express in the national currency of the Contracting State as far as possible the same real value for the amounts in article 6 as is expressed there in units of account. Contracting States must communicate to the depositary the manner of calculation pursuant to paragraph 1 of this article, or the result of the conversion mentioned in paragraph 3 of this article, as the case may be, at the time of signature or when depositing their instruments of ratification, acceptance, approval or accession, or when availing themselves of the option provided for in paragraph 2 of this article and whenever there is a change in the manner of such calculation or in the result of such conversion.

PART VII. FINAL CLAUSES

Article 27. Depositary

The Secretary-General of the United Nations is hereby designated as the depositary of this Convention.

Article 28. Signature, ratification, acceptance, approval, accession

1. This Convention is open for signature by all States until 30 April 1979 at the Headquarters of the United Nations, New York.

2. This Convention is subject to ratification, acceptance or approval by the signatory States.

3. After 30 April 1979, this Convention will be open for accession by all States which are not signatory States.

4. Instruments of ratification, acceptance, approval and accession are to be deposited with the Secretary-General of the United Nations.

Article 29. Reservations

No reservations may be made to this Convention.

Article 30. Entry into force

1. This Convention enters into force on the first day of the month following the expiration of one year from the date of deposit of the 20th instrument of ratification, acceptance, approval or accession.

2. For each State which becomes a Contracting State to this Convention after the date of the deposit of the 20th instrument of ratification, acceptance, approval or accession, this Convention enters into force on the first day of the month following the expiration of one year after the deposit of the appropriate instrument on behalf of that State.

3. Each Contracting State shall apply the provisions of this Convention to contracts of carriage by sea concluded on or after the date of the entry into force of this Convention in respect of that State.

Article 31. Denunciation of other conventions

1. Upon becoming a Contracting State to this Convention, any State party to the International Convention for the Unification of Certain Rules relating to Bills of Lading signed at Brussels on 25 August 1924 (1924 Convention) must notify the Government of Belgium as the depositary of the 1924 Convention of its denunciation of the said Convention with a declaration that the denunciation is to take effect as from the date when this Convention enters into force in respect of that State.

2. Upon the entry into force of this Convention under paragraph 1 of article 30, the depositary of this Convention must notify the Government of Belgium as the depositary of the 1924 Convention of the date of such entry into force, and of the names of the Contracting States in respect of which the Convention has entered into force.

3. The provisions of paragraphs 1 and 2 of this article apply correspondingly in respect of States parties to the Protocol signed on 23 February 1968 to amend the International Convention for

the Unification of Certain Rules relating to Bills of Lading signed at Brussels on 25 August 1924.

4. Notwithstanding article 2 of this Convention, for the purposes of paragraph 1 of this article, a Contracting State may, if it deems it desirable, defer the denunciation of the 1924 Convention and of the 1924 Convention as modified by the 1968 Protocol for a maximum period of five years from the entry into force of this Convention. It will then notify the Government of Belgium of its intention. During this transitory period, it must apply to the Contracting States this Convention to the exclusion of any other one.

Article 32. Revision and amendment

1. At the request of not less than one-third of the Contracting States to this Convention, the depositary shall convene a conference of the Contracting States for revising or amending it.

2. Any instrument of ratification, acceptance, approval or accession deposited after the entry into force of an amendment to this Convention, is deemed to apply to the Convention as amended.

Article 33. Revision of the limitation amounts and unit of account or monetary unit

1. Notwithstanding the provisions of article 32, a conference only for the purpose of altering the amount specified in article 6 and paragraph 2 of article 26, or of substituting either or both of the units defined in paragraphs 1 and 3 of article 26 by other units is to be convened by the depositary in accordance with paragraph 2 of this article. An alteration of the amounts shall be made only because of a significant change in their real value.

2. A revision conference is to be convened by the depositary when not less than one-fourth of the Contracting States so request.

3. Any decision by the conference must be taken by a two-thirds majority of the participating States. The amendment is communicated by the depositary to all the Contracting States for acceptance and to all the States signatories of the Convention for information.

4. Any amendment adopted enters into force on the first day of the month following one year after its acceptance by two-thirds of the Contracting States. Acceptance is to be effected by the deposit of a formal instrument to that effect, with the depositary.

5. After entry into force of an amendment a Contracting State which has accepted the amendment is entitled to apply the Convention as amended in its relations with Contracting States

which have not within six months after the adoption of the amendment notified the depositary that they are not bound by the amendment.

6. Any instrument of ratification, acceptance, approval or accession deposited after the entry into force of an amendment to this Convention, is deemed to apply to the Convention as amended.

Article 34. Denunciation

1. A Contracting State may denounce this Convention at any time by means of a notification in writing addressed to the depositary.

2. The denunciation takes effect on the first day of the month following the expiration of one year after the notification is received by the depositary. Where a longer period is specified in the notification, the denunciation takes effect upon the expiration of such longer period after the notification is received by the depositary.

DONE at Hamburg, this thirty-first day of March one thousand nine hundred and seventy-eight, in a single original, of which the Arabic, Chinese, English, French, Russian and Spanish texts are equally authentic.

IN WITNESS WHEREOF the undersigned plenipotentiaries, being duly authorized by their respective Governments, have signed the present Convention.

ANNEX II
COMMON UNDERSTANDING ADOPTED BY THE UNITED NATIONS CONFERENCE ON THE CARRIAGE OF GOODS BY SEA

It is the common understanding that the liability of the carrier under this Convention is based on the principle of presumed fault or neglect. This means that, as a rule, the burden of proof rests on the carrier but, with respect to certain cases, the provisions of the Convention modify this rule.